Decision Making
in
Disaster Response

Decision Making
in
Disaster Response

Strategies for Frontline Humanitarian Responders

J. S. Tipper

Relief Advisory International
Jasper Avenue, Mount Roskill
Auckland 1041 New Zealand

A catalogue record for this book is available from
Te Puna Mātauranga o Aotearoa
The National Library of New Zealand

ISBN:0473379023
ISBN-13: 978-0-47337-902-5

DEDICATION

I can deal with a lot as I respond to disasters. But I can never resolve all the innocent young lives – street children, orphans and others – that I see neglected and abused and left like litter strewn against the roadside.

And yet there's hope. Selfless, caring, infinitely patient people. Those who put aside their own comfort and live in these bleak places, year in, year out, and slowly, gradually make a difference in these hurt and broken young lives. To all of you who do that work, you're my heroes. This book is dedicated to you and your tireless compassion.

Decision Making in Disaster Response

CONTENTS

Introduction   9

Part One: Building Experience

1   Single Option Decision Making   17

2   Values   36

3   Compromise   64

4   Gifts, Bribes, and Extortion   87

5   Organisational Policies   138

6   Perceptions   160

7   Other Organisations   194

8   Daily Challenges   226

9   Final Guidance   260

Part Two: Theory

10   Making the case for Naturalistic Decision Making   265

11   An Investigation of Real Life Decision Makers   279

12   Implications for Training   287

Endnotes   295

Appendices   303

Decision Making in Disaster Response

INTRODUCTION

At some point you're going to be on your own, faced with an urgent decision. Or you're going to be leading a team, and they're all looking to you, right now, to give a response. The decision you make will be critical. Quite possibly the outcome will affect people's lives. You need to get it right, *right now.*

But here's the thing: despite all the induction that your organisation gave you, despite that degree you might have in development, despite the well-written project plan back in your office – despite all this and more, no-one ever sat you down and taught you how to make decisions – under pressure, serious-consequence decisions – in disaster response.

There's a lot of conventional wisdom out there: take your time, list the options, evaluate them, get more information if you need it, consult with others, and so on. But one limit of conventional wisdom is that it's developed *in* conventional situations, *for* conventional situations. One feature of disaster response is that situations generally aren't conventional. They're anything but. Sure, you might be operating under the convention that as an NGO you have the right to transport certain goods, tax free, through a territory. But the young, uneducated local militia member blocking your way doesn't know that. He knows that he has a gun, and you don't, and in the words of one UN security trainer, "the bottom line is, the man with the gun is always right."

So forget all the option gathering, the discussions, the evaluations, the seeking out of further information. It's you, and your task, and the man with the gun in front of you. What exactly are you going to do? How do you arrive at that decision? How do you know it's the right decision? What impact will that decision have on those who come after you? What is your agency going to say about your decision?

The chances are that no-one ever got alongside you and took the time to help you develop a plan for these kinds of situations. If you've been fortunate enough, you've been through similar situations with more experienced colleagues. You've seen how they handle them, and you've learned a few skills and developed some good instincts. You might have got to know a particular situation well, and learned how to navigate those local challenges very competently. But what happens if you haven't had good mentoring or much experience? Or if you've moved across the world to a new disaster situation, one where the cultural norms are very different?

The reality is, in disaster response situations, you're going to be operating in very challenging situations. Think for a minute of a large-scale typhoon which has caused great damage. You may only have limited information about the situation itself, since the circumstances are new and continue to change. Your overall goal may not be clear, or you may even be working to reach several competing goals. The resources at your disposal may be inadequate, and you may be desperately understaffed. The presence of many other individuals and organisations, all with their own goals, may have an additional impact on your actions. In the midst of all this complexity, and under significant pressure, you will be forced to make decision after decision.

That's where this book comes in, to help you make good decisions in disaster response. To get away from conventional wisdom, and to develop your skill in making decisions when it really counts. To make decisions that will help save lives, decisions that will help your colleagues to do their jobs well, decisions that you'll sleep comfortably about.

Let's start with an extremely quick overview. If you want to know more, there's a whole section at the end that shows why this book's approach to decision making is more suited to disaster response than the methods that are usually suggested. But that's where the discussion belongs: at the end. Once you've used this method a bit, tried it out, come to your own conclusions – that's the time to review the theory.

The single most helpful author on decision making for people working at the frontline in disaster response is the psychologist Dr Gary Klein. Dr Klein writes about a body of theory called Naturalistic Decision Making. Within this field he promotes a specific methodology that he calls Recognition-Primed Decision Making, or RPD.

In short, Recognition-Primed Decision Making looks like this:

- Encounter a situation
- Recognise the type of situation
- Use experience to suggest a particular, *single* solution
- Mentally evaluate the solution
- Will it work? Yes – then apply the solution
- Yes it will work, except for one glitch? Okay, adapt the solution to overcome the glitch
- Will the adapted version work? Yes – apply the solution
- Yes the adapted version will work, except for one glitch? Okay, adapt the solution again to overcome the new glitch
- Will the new adapted version work? Yes – then apply the solution
- No, it won't work? Okay, discard the solution, use experience to suggest a second solution
- Now go through the review process again
- And so on, until an acceptable solution is found.

If you want to know more about the theory in depth, with lots of helpful, illustrative stories, Dr Klein's book – "Sources of Power: How People Make Decisions" [1] – can be found for sale at many major online book retailers. It is highly recommended reading for anyone working under conditions of high pressure in humanitarian disaster response.

There are two points which are central to the Recognition-Primed Decision Making approach. The first is *experience,* leading to *pattern recognition*. The decision maker uses their experience to recognise a particular pattern in the situation, in order to bring a solution to mind. Without that experience the process falls apart.

The second key point is that solutions are generated one at a time, and *only as many as are needed.* If the first solution did the job, what was the point in building up several other solutions? There was no time for it anyway. These are not slow, lazy decisions with lots of time in hand. They're time-pressured, immediate decision points.

Practising decision making

The aim of this book is for you to get lots of practice, to build up your level of experience in common disaster response situations. Think of it like spending hours in a flight simulator practising emergency landings: it's not the real thing but it will equip you to handle the real thing should it arise.

Also, you're going to practise generating one option at a time. That's critical. If you find yourself comparing options, you've missed the point.

As you work your way through the examples that make up this book, try to remember that you are not looking for the 'best' decision. You are looking for the first solution which is good enough. This is the most vital concept to grasp:

"Is this solution good enough?" Yes? Then go with the choice.

These are not situations where there is time to sit around and generate a lot of options and select the best one. If the first solution that comes to mind is great, then that's very good. But if the first solution that comes to mind is good enough, then that's also perfectly acceptable. Act on it, and move on.

As you progress through the book, the scenarios will build up and reinforce the learning from previous chapters. Remember, the aim is to build up expertise. The more familiar you are with a situation, the less foreign it will feel when you actually encounter it. In some cases you will begin to build up your familiarity to the point where you can see patterns in the outcomes.

Decision making in high-pressured situations is not an exact science but rather an art form. It may involve balancing some competing priorities. Even very experienced decision makers may respond in different ways in quite similar situations. By practising your decision making through the pages of this book, you'll be better equipped to make solid, effective decisions when faced with the real thing.

PART ONE :

BUILDING EXPERIENCE

CHAPTER ONE

SINGLE OPTION
DECISION MAKING

Over the course of the book you'll build up your experience at decision points. You'll become familiar with some of the most common challenges in disaster response, and build up an understanding of appropriate solutions. But experience is only part of the Recognition-Primed Decision Making approach. The second key part is that you only generate solutions one at a time, and that you stop the moment you reach a solution that is good enough. In the decision points that you encounter in this chapter, your goal is to practise this single-solution approach.

How it works:

First read the brief chapter introduction. This will describe the principles you will focus on during the chapter.

After the chapter introduction, a particular scenario will be described. As you read through the scenario you will be faced with a problem, and a series of decision points

At each decision point you will be presented with one possible solution. Your task is to take that suggested solution and tell yourself the story of what you think will happen next, as a result of applying that solution. At this point, work hard to avoid getting into comparisons. Try to stay focused on the first choice being presented to you. Play the story forward in your mind, imagining what could happen.

You have three possible next steps:

- If you like the possible outcome of the suggested solution – the story you have told yourself – select "Yes."

- If you like the possible outcome but are concerned about certain things not working well, select "Maybe." You may then be presented with a modified version of the solution. You can choose to keep it, or…

- If you don't like the initial solution, or the modified solution, you are guided onto a different suggestion. You should only move onto this second option if you didn't like the mental outcome of the first option.

To get the most from this training, try to discipline yourself not to go back to an option you've already dismissed.

This is to stop you revealing all the possible options, and then selecting between them. Remember that the RPD approach does not compare options, it just takes the first solution that is good enough.

Once you've been through all the problems in the scenario, you'll reach the teaching section. This will provide feedback on the scenario, and describe how certain principles can be recognised and applied in order to improve your decision-making skills.

Make use of the 'principles' page at the end of each chapter. Write down any principles which occur to you based on your learning in the chapter. These principles will help guide you when it comes to making actual decisions, so keep them short, memorable and useable.

Finally, having studied the teaching material, and with your own principles in mind, run through the chapter's exercises a second time. If you were not completely fixed on your choice of solution try starting with a different option. Work through the scenario, taking the chance to apply the feedback and your principles.

Scenario One

The civil war has been going on for several months now. At first it was fairly clear who was fighting: the main opposition group were targeting government soldiers when they drove out into the countryside. Recently other groups have joined the conflict. Some of them appear to support the opposition, and others seem focused on robberies, carjackings, and general banditry. Other groups are made up of a few troops loyal to a particular commander, who have switched sides in support of the opposition. It has become less and less clear who is who, and which places are still safe.

Out of fear of the conflict, many people have left their small, isolated villages and are now spread out along the highways into town. They have erected tarpaulins and other rough forms of shelter, and are too afraid to return to the villages. Many of them have fled with very little, and can no longer afford food or medicine. A shortage of supplies in the town has driven up the prices of the remaining goods, and many foods are no longer available.

You're in charge of a small team running food distribution to the families now stranded on these highways. You operate with the government's permission, and your supply base is a town several kilometres away across the desert, where goods are readily available. You usually drive out to bring food to the displaced villagers, and then return to your own base before nightfall.

You are in a three-vehicle convoy consisting of two single-cabin pickup trucks and a nine-seater four-wheel drive. As the team coordinator you are the front passenger in the 4WD, at the head of the group. Your group does not have long-range radios fitted in the vehicles, but you do have a small handheld radio in each vehicle, with an effective range of about 2km.

Evening is fast approaching, and you have one more stop to make outside a small school, to give out the remaining food items. You've planned this distribution with the school's headmaster. You know people are hungry but you're very concerned to finish quickly. The road across the desert can be very dangerous at night, with many bandit attacks on vehicles. You realise that you don't have long to finish your task safely.

As you approach the school, you notice a number of armed soldiers sitting on the steps. From their uniforms and weapons you can't identify which group they belong to.

The soldiers stand up as you approach.

Do you keep driving in order to reassess from a safe distance?

Yes: go to 1

Otherwise go to 2

1 You don't like the idea of being caught up in a situation when it's unclear who the soldiers are or what they want. You quickly tell your driver to continue down the road, knowing that the other vehicles will follow your lead.

As your vehicle drives past, some of the soldiers run out onto the road. Your vehicle and the first pickup truck are already past them, but you can see in your mirror that the soldiers have blocked the second truck from passing. As you drive along the road it rapidly becomes smaller in your mirror. You can see that several soldiers have surrounded it.

Do you drive on a clear distance and try to contact the second pickup truck by handheld radio?

Yes: go to 3

Otherwise go to 4

2 You slow down and turn into the dirt space in front of the school. Two of the soldiers approach your 4WD, while the others step across towards the pickup trucks. In the vehicle's side mirror you see some soldiers lifting the tarpaulin that covers one of the trucks.

Do you climb out of the vehicle and go to where the soldiers are opening the truck cover?

Yes: go to 5

Otherwise go to 6

3 Your vehicle and the first pickup truck turn a bend in the road and then pull into an abandoned petrol station. You switch your radio on and try to call the second pickup truck. But there is no reply. "They probably won't answer, or the soldiers will think that they're spies," your driver says.

You quickly discuss the situation with your colleagues in your vehicle. Some people think you should go back, some think you should wait.

Do you decide to all go back to support the second truck?

Yes: go to 9

Maybe: go to 10

Otherwise go to 13

4 You turn your two vehicles around and go back to where the other pickup truck has been halted by soldiers. On closer inspection you can see that the soldiers are in fact fire brigade. Their camouflaged uniform looks very similar to soldiers, but you notice the distinctive red dots.
An agitated-looking older man in camouflage approaches your window.

"One of my men is badly burned," he says. "We need you to take a look."

Do you agree to take a look at the injured man?

Yes: go to 7   **Otherwise go to 8**

5 You climb out of your vehicle and start moving towards the rear trucks. Through the windscreen of the first truck, you see the driver looks alarmed. You don't know if it is at your behaviour or for another reason.

Suddenly a soldier steps out from between the vehicles. "Where do you think you're going? The chief wants to talk to you." Before you realise, he's caught you by the arm, and bundled you round to the front of your own vehicle, where an older soldier is waiting.

Go to 6

6 You find yourself face to face with a senior official. On closer inspection you can see that he and his soldiers are in fact from the fire brigade. In their camouflaged uniform they look very similar to soldiers, but you notice the distinctive red dots in the pattern.

The official looks at you with worry on his face. "One of my men is badly burned," he says. "We need you to take a look."

Do you agree to take a look at the injured man?

Yes: go to 7

Otherwise go to 8

7 You follow the commander towards the tree. Your colleague who is a nurse follows right behind you.

You see a man propped against the base of a tree, moaning in pain. His left arm is very badly burned. It's clear that he needs a hospital, but the only one is in your home town. You explain this to the commander.

"I see. Well then I need you to take him and two others to care for him."

You glance at the sky and see that there is not much daylight left.

Do you agree, but insist on distributing the food first, knowing it will take at least 30 minutes?

Yes: go to 14   Otherwise go to 18

8 You explain that you are not a medical professional. The commander brushes your objections aside.

"I know about NGOs, I've seen all the hospitals. You all know what you're doing."

"Well I can't make any promises," you say. "But I can have a look. My colleague is a nurse. Can she come with us?"

"Yes, of course," the commander replies.

He beckons you towards the shade of a large tree.

Go to 7

9 When you reach the armed group your colleague comes up to your vehicle. With her is a worried-looking man, who she introduces as the group's commander. You notice the red markings on his uniform, indicating that he is with the fire brigade. You feel yourself relax, as the fire brigade has a very solid reputation.

The commander greets you briefly, and gets right to the point. "We really need your help," he explains. "We were dealing with a house fire, and a burning beam trapped my man's arm. He needs urgent treatment." You follow the commander towards the shade of a huge, ancient tree. You see a man propped against the base of a tree, moaning in pain. His left arm is very badly burned. It's clear that he needs a hospital, but the only one is in your home town.

"Our vehicle has a problem," the commander tells you. "We can't move him anywhere. We see you've got several vehicles, can you take him for us?"

Moving through the crowd that has gathered around the tree, you manage to take a brief look at the man's arm. He needs such urgent attention that you decide to go immediately. As the injured man is loaded on top of the food packs in the pickup truck, you hear a lot of grumbling from the crowd.

Do you gather together a few local people, and give them the food to distribute, even though you have no way of knowing who will receive the food?

Yes: go to 17

Otherwise go to 18

10 You turn to the rest of your team and explain that you will go back with the first pickup truck, and ask them to wait with the 4WD. One of your team asks if they can just drive straight back to your base town, rather than sit waiting.

He suggests that they can inform the UN security department about your problem with the soldiers.

Do you ask the vehicle to remain where it is, with the radio on, until you find out more?

Yes: go to 11

Otherwise go to 12

11 As you pass the handheld radio to your colleague, it suddenly crackles with static. Then you hear a clear voice.

"It's okay to come back. There's no problem, they just want our help with an injured colleague."

You trust your colleague on the radio. She has been in the area for several months and you've witnessed her good judgement before.

You explain to your colleagues that you will all be going back to where you saw the soldiers, and that you plan to continue with the distribution. **Go to 9**

12

You agree to let the first vehicle return to your base town. But then a small voice inside makes you pause. You remember that you have strict instructions to stay in convoy. Also, you realise, you don't even know enough about the problem to know if you should involve UN security.

Suddenly your radio crackles into life. "It's okay to come back. There's no problem at all, they just want our help with an injured colleague."

You explain to your colleagues that you will all be going back to where you saw the soldiers, and that you plan to continue with the distribution. **Go to 9**

13

You decide to pause for a few minutes and see what develops, rather than rush into potential trouble and make the situation worse.

The handheld radio suddenly crackles with static. Then you hear a clear voice.

"It's okay to come back. There's no problem, they just want our help with an injured colleague."

You trust your colleague on the radio. She has been in the area for several months and you've witnessed her good judgement before. You explain to your colleagues that you will all be going back to where you saw the soldiers, and that you plan to continue with the distribution. **Go to 9**

14
You explain that you must consider the welfare of the people needing food as well.

"Okay," the commander accepts. "But I don't want my man to suffer for long. Let me order my men to help you with the food distribution."

You're aware of the fast approaching night, the danger on the road after dark, and the injured man's needs.

However, your team has worked quickly and efficiently at the other distributions and you don't think this one will take long.

Do you accept the offer of help from the uniformed, armed men?

Yes: go to 15

Otherwise go to 16

15 With the help of the uniformed group you hurriedly start offloading the food parcels and carrying them into the school for further distribution.

You notice that the headmaster is quite reserved when he greets you, and also that most of the neighbourhood people also hang back. The whole atmosphere feels a bit odd, but you can't describe exactly what it is you are feeling. This is quite different to what you experienced at the earlier distributions, where people were friendly and welcoming. You wonder if the fire brigade are as well respected as you first thought.

The injured man is quickly loaded into the truck along with his two colleagues. You are relieved to see that they leave their weapons behind. All three of your vehicles drive out of town towards your home town, as the last of the light starts to fade.
Ends.

16 You explain that you have to be careful about how your organisation is perceived by the people it is serving, and that you prefer to keep a distinction between yourselves and the official's group. He tells his men just to focus on putting the burned man in the truck while your team carries the food parcels into the school.

The local headmaster and the group of people surrounding him are all very friendly and helpful as they join you in unloading the goods. The headmaster insists on going with you to the edge of his town to say goodbye. You leave him at the edge of town as day is fading, and are soon safely across the desert in your own town. **Ends.**

17 You start to pick out a few people from the crowd to take the food boxes. As you do, the local headmaster comes up to the truck with several other people.

"Leave it to us," he says. "We'll make sure those that need it most get the food." You've worked with him before and trust him. Relieved, you turn your attention to the injured man.

The burned man's two colleagues are climbing into the truck with him. You notice they still have their guns with them. You've seen most aid vehicles in the area have "No Weapons" stickers on the doors.

However, you're quite concerned that you're going to be driving through the desert almost at night.

Do you insist that the men on the truck leave all their weapons behind?

Yes: go to 19

Otherwise go to 20

18

You hear your colleague calling out to the crowd. The grumbling decreases, and she comes back to you.

"I told them that this is one group that they really want on their side," she explains. "They can see the reason in that. I told them that we'll be back first thing in the morning."

The burned man's two colleagues are starting to get into the truck with him. You notice they still have their guns with them. You've seen most aid vehicles in the area have "No Weapons" stickers on the doors.

However, you're quite concerned that you're going to be driving through the desert almost at night.

Do you allow the men to carry their weapons with them?

Yes: go to 20

Otherwise go to 19

19

You explain that you simply are not allowed by your agency to carry weapons on your vehicles.

"But it's a dangerous drive across that desert," the two armed men protest. "How can we protect you if we leave our weapons behind?"

However, you insist and finally their commander tells them to leave their weapons with him.

It's almost dark as you set off across the desert. The 30-minute drive seems to last a lot longer, and you find yourselves expecting armed bandits around every curve.

Finally you reach your base town and drive the injured man straight to the Red Cross hospital. **Ends.**

20

You allow the two men to carry their weapons with them, and ask one of them to join you in the front vehicle, so that your convoy will have some protection through the desert at night.

After a half-hour drive through the desert you reach your base town, and drive straight to the Red Cross hospital.

As you are dropping off the injured man and his colleagues at the entrance, two foreign aid workers who you don't recognise come up to you.

"You know, it makes it so much harder for us to insist on no weapons when some aid workers carry armed men in their vehicles," one of them says. **Ends.**

Single option decision making

The main goal of this first chapter is to build your familiarity with a single option decision. Don't be too concerned if you're not happy with the outcome of your choice. Firstly, the story presented is a limited model – in real life you would have more chances to modify your solution, and secondly, the aim is for you to become comfortable generating a solution which is *good enough* – and then move on.

It is important to remember that there is rarely a 'right' decision in disaster response. Many times you are faced with an impossible set of choices. In order to be effective you should do *something*. For example, you might be familiar with the concept of 'do no harm'. There's a risk that this memorable catchphrase becomes adopted into a goal, whereas real life rarely falls into such a neat distinction. In the final instance, it is often better to make a decision which is good enough, which *on balance* does more good than harm, than to submit to a state of paralysis that does nothing of value while it looks in vain for a 'no harm' option. In a similar way, most choices have positive and negative components associated with them. Becoming a better decision maker under pressure involves becoming comfortable with a 'good enough' mindset.

As you get into subsequent chapters you'll encounter suggestions, tips, guidance, all of which will build your ability to make a good decision. Certain choices will be presented as generally more preferable than others. But in this first scenario, there isn't specific feedback on your choices. The main goal is just to become familiar with the 'good enough, one option at a time' approach.

As you build your experience in subsequent chapters, don't be drawn back into making *comparative* decisions. There is a place for that in disaster response, but it's for situations where there's more time available to gather information and evaluate options, where you can consult with colleagues, where you can look to your agency for guidance, or where you are making a collective decision with other organisations. The RPD method is for you, when you're on your own or under pressure to make a quick decision, *without* all the peripheral support just mentioned.

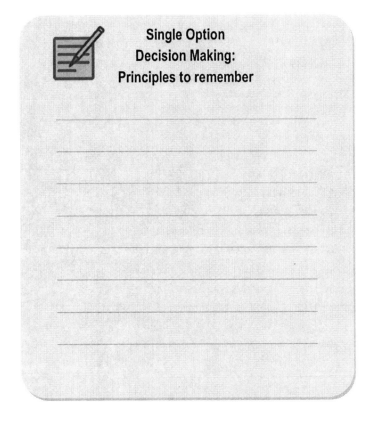

Single Option Decision Making: Principles to remember

CHAPTER TWO

VALUES

This chapter looks at the role that values play in guiding our decisions. Our own personal and cultural values play a role, and the values of the organisation we represent also affect our decisions. Furthermore, there are values that many humanitarian workers uphold and are guided by, and knowing these will also influence our choices.

Many of the decisions that we encounter in disaster response have an element of moral choice involved. The front-line of decision making is not the place to discover our values. To perform well under stress, it will help if we take time to reflect on our own values, in advance of the actual high-pressure situation.

Scenario Two

Ethnic-based fighting has caused thousands of people to flee their part of Central Asia. There is a huge surge of refugees, people who have left their own country but who don't feel safe in the neighbouring one. Most of them are trying to transit through this neighbouring country to reach a third country by the southern coast, where they share ethnicity with a large part of the population.

The scale and speed at which the crisis has developed has caught almost everyone by surprise. To make it worse, aid agencies are spread very thin responding to a civil war in Southeast Asia and the devastating effects of a recent earthquake in the Middle East. Very little funding is available, and many skilled, experienced staff are already deployed elsewhere.

Thankfully, an unusually large contingent of volunteers has become involved, using private donations raised mainly through social media campaigning. Groups of volunteers are working independently but some individuals are joining organisations like yours, in order to be part of a more established operation. Many of them have no experience of disaster response but they are committed, hard-working, and genuinely care for the refugees they encounter.

You're leading a small team in this transit country. You're part of a tent village at a bleak, mountainous point where the train line finishes and people are forced to walk several hours on tracks to reach a bus station a town across the mountain. Many of the people you're serving are completely unprepared for the harsh mountain climate. Their clothing is inadequate, and the night-time drop in temperature makes hypothermia an ever-present risk. Lower down the mountain is a large trading town, with a large range of goods. Unfortunately for the refugees the train doesn't stop at this town, and from those who have walked down to it, there are stories of the town's police treating them very badly. As a result, most refugees start on the mountain trek as soon as they possibly can. Only those who are unable to keep moving spend time in the transit camp. As a result, most agencies, including your own, are focused on providing people with food, warm clothing and basic medical supplies.

The lady volunteering to run the clothing tent approaches you. A donor has given some money that they want to be specifically used to help women, since so much of the news, and the resulting support, is focused on the needs of children.

"I got some prices last time I was down in the town," she says. "I'm focusing on headscarves because World Aid have got a good supply of warm coats to give out. These ladies are really stuck. Their scarves are wet and dirty, but they can't take them off in public. Most of them are from really conservative backgrounds.

"I have enough for about one hundred and fifty scarves. But they're really basic quality. I mean, they'll do the job, but the quality, the designs..." her voice tails off. "What I really want to do is get these better scarves. They've got a much nicer weave, they're warmer, and they really have a good-quality feel to them. But even with a discount, I can only get about ninety for the money. What should I do?"

Do you tell her to get the better quality scarves?
Yes: go to 1   Otherwise go to 2

1

That evening you're standing outside the clothing tent, checking the night schedule with another volunteer, a young man who left his university course to come to volunteer. You notice your colleague who bought the scarves inside the tent, talking with a middle-aged lady. The lady has three children near her. She seems really happy, and her hand constantly strokes the new headscarf she's wearing. As she leaves the clothing tent she stops to give your colleague a long hug.

A moment later your colleague comes up to you. There are tears in her eyes.

"She said that's the first time she's felt like she's worth something since she left home. Two months of feeling like rubbish that no-one wants, and finally she feels human again. I'm so glad we got those better scarves. It's amazing what a small thing can do. That's the fifth woman who's stopped and talked with me." She walks away towards the supply tent.

The young man next to you watches as the mother and her children walk towards the mountain track.

"I didn't want to say this in front of her," he says, motioning to the supply tent, "because she's really well-meaning. But what happens when those ninety scarves are gone? There'll be another sixty people going across that mountain with wet scarves on, because she wanted to get the more expensive scarves. I just don't think this is the time to be focused on making people feel special. We have to do the bare basics for as many as we can."

Go to 3

2 That evening you're standing outside the clothing tent, checking the night schedule with another volunteer, a young man who left his university course to come to volunteer. You notice your colleague who bought the scarves inside the tent, talking with a middle-aged lady. The lady has three children near her. She yells at the children, telling them to be still while she fiddles with her headscarf. Grabbing the smallest by the back of the coat, she pulls her towards the edge of the tent.

Your colleague comes up to you. There are tears in her eyes.

"I can't stand to see those children treated so roughly. The mums are just so harsh with them. I wish I could find a way to get through to them, to help them deal with all the stress. But they all just rush through." She walks away towards the supply tent.

The young man next to you watches as the mother and her children walk towards the mountain track.

"I didn't want to say this in front of her," he says, motioning to the supply tent, "because she's clearly so bothered by what she sees. But I just don't think this is the time to be focused on making people feel special. We have to keep people alive and hope they get to where they're going. There'll be time there for them to get their lives together and stop stressing so much."

Go to 3

3   Later that night, during a lull between incoming trains, you sit back in the clothing tent and enjoy the rare chance to get a few minutes' rest. The boxes full of canned food you're sitting on aren't comfy, but you've been on your feet for hours and the break feels great.

An older couple come into the tent. They've been volunteering for the last few nights. Her skills as a nurse have been extremely useful, and his calm, patient manner reflect his years as a special needs teacher.

The lady spots you and comes over. "We want to follow up with that family that came in at lunch time, before our shift starts again. You know, the ones who had that boy in the wheelchair. They said they were staying to rest. Simon found them a cushion that will make the wheelchair more comfortable. Do you know where they are?"

So much for the break, you think. The camp is so haphazard, it's hard to describe where anything is. You decide it's easier to show them yourself.

You step out into the cold air. A light mist hangs low to the ground, and the tents are all beaded with moisture. Stepping carefully between guy ropes, you lead them to a cluster of tents at the base of an embankment. Off to one side a group of men stand huddled against the cold, the faint ember of lit cigarettes casting a weak glow in the darkness. One of the tents is larger than the others, the entrance door zipped down tight to the ground.

"As far as I know, they're in here," you say, stepping forwards. **Do you go in to check the tent?**

Yes: go to 4   **Otherwise go to 5**

41

4 You step into the tent, followed by the older couple. Several people are seated on the ground. Immediately they scrabble around them for their headscarves, pulling them up over their heads. A moment later several men burst in behind you. You turn round and find yourself face to face.

You can't tell what they're saying but they're very angry. Open handed, you try to explain why you are there. You point to the cushion, and the wheelchair.

One heavily bearded man is furious. He points at the women and then at Simon. A younger man behind him starts to translate:

"He says it's forbidden for you to look at his daughters. You can't come in his tent. You need to leave right now."

For a moment you think of fetching the camp police, so they can remind him of who makes the rules in the camp. But you realise the risk – the man would probably be beaten, and in turn he'd later beat his daughters. You realise the best thing is just to leave. Taking Simon by the arm, you move past the men and step outside. You hear the zip pulled shut behind you. **Go to 12**

5 "Hold on a moment," you tell Simon. "There were ladies in that group. We can't just go stepping in to their tent."

Do you look for male relatives?

Yes: go to 6

Otherwise go to 7

6 You approach the group of men. Cheap tobacco smells waft towards you. Greeting them, you explain who you are and point to the plastic-wrapped cushion that Simon is carrying. Gesturing for your group to wait, one of the men breaks off from the group and heads to the tent. Unzipping the door and ducking low, he steps out of sight.

He reappears a moment later and beckons you to join him. You step into the tent. The gloom is intense, but you make out the shape of a youth huddled in a wheelchair in front of you. Several ladies sit off to one side on a mat on the floor. Pulling up a second mat near the wheelchair, the man gestures for you to sit down.

You all sit down and try to communicate. Your conversation consists mainly of gestures, but you can see that the family appreciates the cushion, and the thoughtfulness behind it.

Just as you think you should be getting back to work, one of the men enters the tent with a pack of biscuits and three cups of tea. You realise he must have fetched the tea from the cooking tent, but you know that the camp ran out of biscuits several hours ago. These biscuits must have come from the food pack the family were given on arrival.

As he offers the tea and biscuits to you, you can't help but think of the sandwiches you have wrapped in your bag in your vehicle. You know this family won't get anything else to eat until they pass through the mountains. Pushing a wheelchair over that track is going to exhaust them.

Do you try to show that you can't take the biscuits, that you have your own food elsewhere?

Yes: go to 8   Otherwise go to 9

7 As you stand there, a harried-looking man in a safari vest runs up. The vest is plastered with agency logos, strung with different radios and medical pouches, and jiggles with every step he takes.

"We've got a full truck of supplies, but the driver says he's leaving in ten minutes. We need everyone in camp to help unload it. Can you get all your people to help? We're at the front gate."

He runs off into the maze of tents.

"The cushion will have to wait," you tell your colleagues. "We really need these supplies. Let's go help unload this truck."

Go to 12

8 You try to explain that you have your own food elsewhere. The family insist, but you manage to keep refusing. You know how much they will need the food.

Finally the message seems to get through. But you notice the atmosphere change. It's subtle, but you sense a shift. You drink the warm, sweet tea and decide you really must be going.

Thanking them again for the offer of the food, you stand up, duck through the entrance and leave the tent.

Go to 12

9 You accept the pack of biscuits that is offered to you. Taking one, you pass the packet over to your colleagues.

After spending a few more minutes drinking tea you decide you have to be going. The youth in the wheelchair reaches out to thank you, and two of the men accompany you outside.

As you walk back towards the clothing tent you remember the emergency supplies that the local doctor has. You've been helping each other out in different ways for the last few days. The local culture runs on exchanging favours, and you've tried hard to make sure you've helped people more than they've helped you. You know how useful it can be when people feel they owe you some help.

You're sure the doctor would spare a couple of packets of high energy biscuits if you asked her. But you're mindful of how much you ask her for. You never know what emergency will arise that will need help.

Do you send Simon over to ask the doctor for some biscuits, to pass on quietly to the family?

Yes: go to 10

Otherwise go to 11

10 You explain the situation to Simon. He heads off to the doctor's tent.

Later that evening you see him again, passing out cups of tea at the food tent. He tells you that he was able to give the biscuits to the boy's father, and explain how hard the journey would be. He says that the father took the biscuits and thanked him.

Go to 12

11 You decide it's really important to have the doctor's cooperation when you need it, and not spoil it by asking for too many small favours.

"I need a few minutes before I start at the food tent," Simon tells you. "I have some chocolate bars in the car. I can't think of that family going through the mountains with no food. They won't make it, they need energy." He leaves towards the barren field where the volunteers park their cars.

As he leaves, you wonder what he thinks of your leadership. Should you have been the one to notice the family's needs? You push the thought to the back of your mind and return to work.

Go to 12

12 Later that night you stand by the food tent, handing out cups of steaming, sweet tea. The temperature has plummeted, and almost everyone who hurries past is shivering. Cups of tea are gratefully taken from you and the other volunteers. Inside the tent, the other side of a wooden trestle table, a volunteer brews another huge pot of tea on a gas stove. You watch as he tips a whole bag of sugar into the pot.

You turn around with more drinks to hand out, and find yourself faced with a young mother. Her eyes are dull and vacant. Another young lady, maybe a sister, is rearranging a bundle of clothing strapped to her front. The bundle wriggles slightly, and you realise there's a baby in there.

The lady holds up four fingers, showing you she needs tea for her and three others. You realise some is for the children, and you pause to cool the piping hot tea with some cold water so that the children don't burn their lips.

The lady with the baby holds out a small bottle. You see that there's milk powder at the bottom. Your colleague takes it, and hunts around for the thermos of hot water you keep for filling bottles. After filling the bottle, your colleague pours a drop on her hand to check it isn't too hot. Then she passes it back to the mother. Instead of taking it, the lady points to where your colleague is making tea. After a moment's confusion, you all realise that she wants to get to one of the large bags of sugar on the tea table.

"Hey!" your colleague calls, "I've seen this last night. These people put whole spoons of sugar in the baby milk. We can't let her do that to her baby's milk. It's so unhealthy."
Do you give her the sugar?
Yes: go to 13   Otherwise go to 14

13

You decide it's not your role to decide what's right for someone's child. None of you are nutritionists, and the situation is clearly an emergency. Keeping the baby warm is more important to you than whether or not you should be giving sugar. You reach across for the bag of sugar and a spoon. The young mother spoons two large helpings into the bottle, then shakes it hard. Herding the children in front of them, the two ladies walk off down the dark trail.

Your colleague is furious. "We're promoting such appalling practices. I can't believe we're encouraging this. You're the leader. You should be setting an example, not acting like this." **Go to 15**

14

You can't willingly pour lots of sugar into the baby's milk. You shake your head at the mother, and hand her the bottle.

She gets really upset and starts yelling at you. The volunteer making the tea turns around to see what the noise is about. Catching his eye, the lady points pleadingly at the sugar. Without pausing, he takes an empty plastic cup, tips in some sugar and plants a spoon in the small pile. He steps forwards and hands it to the lady. Her yelling stops immediately, and she turns and herds her children away up the track.

The volunteer looks at you. "We get this all the time. It's how they feed their babies. We're here to help, not to impose our values on them. At least the baby will have something warm to drink this way."

Your other colleague is furious. "We're promoting such appalling practices. I can't believe we're encouraging this." **Go to 15**

15 Later on, in the small hours of the morning, you find yourself standing behind a high counter, managing the clothing distribution store. A huddle of people on the other side of the counter try on different coats for size. Next to them a queue stretches out of the front entrance. A volunteer at the entrance tries to limit the surge of people trying to get in. Two others work with you, handing over coats, woolen hats and shoes and taking back those that don't appear to fit. Behind you, three volunteers work endlessly to reorder the piles of tried and discarded clothing onto roughly assembled shelves.

You duck under the counter, push through the crowd and step outside to judge the size of the queue. It snakes out of sight around the corner. People bump against you from the constant shoving behind them. Scanning the crowd, you see plenty of children amongst the adults. Some are just wearing t-shirts. The night-time air is damp and very cold. People are shivering; you hear teeth chattering.

You step back inside and watch those trying on coats. You notice that most people are going through three or four coats before they keep one. But the issue isn't size. You realise they are exchanging coats for different ones the same size, looking for a style that they prefer. You think about your colleague distributing headscarves, who tried to show you the value of helping people keep their dignity. But you also think of those standing outside, shivering.

Do you allow the people at the counter to try two or three different coats?

Yes: go to 16   Maybe: go to 17   Otherwise: go to 20

16
You continue with the system as it is, hoping that people will find something they like.

After a few minutes, you hear more shouting. As you move towards the door, you realise a surge of people are about to force their way into the tent. You're really concerned about the crush. The volunteer at the door panics. He grabs the last few people in the tent and forces them out. Then he slams the door shut.

"We had to do this before," he shouts. "We keep it closed for half an hour until the crowd disappears, and then we can re-open."

You worry that rather than disappear, the crowd may try to force their way in, making things worse.

Do you reopen the tent immediately and enforce stricter rules?

Yes: go to 20   Otherwise go to 21

17
Although you see the value in giving people their dignity, you worry about the really cold children. In the pressure to get clothing, people seem to be ignoring the needs of other people's children. You find this worrying, for your impression to date is that children are generally well cared for in this fairly communal society.

Do you start a separate queue for families with children?

Yes: go to 18   Otherwise go to 19

18 You realise that you have to find a way to prioritize the children. Taking a colleague with you, you shout and gesture to the crowd that families need to come to one side. As people begin to understand, the queue breaks up and starts to rearrange. But the pushing and shoving becomes worse. People start trying to force their way in. Your colleague looks really concerned. "They're going to crush people if we're not careful. We have to move people through more quickly."

You realise that they are right. Calling out over the noise in the tent, you tell all the volunteers that it's now an emergency. People get what they're given. If it fits reasonably well that's good enough. You assign two volunteers to stand in front of the counter and check those trying on clothes, to make sure they don't give back clothes that actually fit.

You hear complaining and grumbling from the people trying on coats; a few try to thrust back the clothing they don't want, but your volunteers stand firm.

After about twenty minutes you realise that people are cycling through the tent much more quickly. You step back outside to check the queue. To your surprise, only about ten people are left outside the tent. The sense of pushing and shoving has dropped right off.

You step back into the tent, duck under the counter, and start to help the volunteers to arrange the discarded clothing.

Ends.

19 You worry about the confusion you'll cause if you have separate queues. You decide to stick to one queue, but you decide to put someone outside to control things better.

You look back at your volunteers and think who you could choose. One of your colleagues is kind and compassionate, and always seems to have a calming word to say to people. She's worked hard to learn some of the local phrases from the refugees that she's encountered so far. However, you have seen a few occasions where men in the crowd only seem to respond to the instructions of other men. You wonder if you should use her to try to control the crowd.
Do you assign her to the outside?

Yes: go to 22   Otherwise go to 23

20 Calling out over the noise in the tent, you tell all the volunteers that it's now an emergency. People get what they're given. If it fits reasonably well that's good enough. You assign two volunteers to stand in front of the counter and check those trying on clothes, to make sure they don't give back clothes that actually fit.

You hear complaining and grumbling from the people trying on coats; a few try to thrust back the clothing they don't want, but your volunteers stand firm.

After about twenty minutes you realise that people are cycling through the tent much more quickly. You step back outside to check the queue. To your surprise, only about ten people are left outside the tent. The sense of pushing and shoving has dropped right off. You step back into the tent, duck under the counter, and start to help the volunteers to arrange the discarded clothing. **Ends.**

21 You decide that you need to keep the clothing building closed for a while to let the crowd disappear. When you explain this to the team inside they are really vocal in their opposition.

"We're here to serve people," one team member points out. "They really need this clothing."

"We just need to manage it better," another agrees. "We can't just shut down because someone got frightened."

"We can manage inside," another adds. "We'll stop giving people any choice in their clothing, and make sure they just take something and leave. We just need a good level of control before people get in."

You decide that they have a point. By being proactive about the crowd and the amount of time that people spend inside, you feel you can continue to deliver a service. You realise you need someone suitable outside the tent to sort the process out before people enter.

You look back at your volunteers and think who you could choose. One of your colleagues is kind and compassionate, and always seems to have a calming word to say to people. She's worked hard to learn some of the local phrases from the refugees that she's encountered so far. However, you have seen a few occasions where men in the crowd only seem to respond to the instructions of other men. You also worry about the surging crowd that you just locked out. You wonder if you should use her presence to try to control the crowd.

Do you assign her to the outside?
Yes: go to 22   Otherwise go to 23

22 You think that your colleague's calming manner might be just what's needed to control the chaos outside. You ask her to try. She agrees, then pulls on a raincoat and steps outside.

You hear muffled sounds outside the tent, but you can't really tell what's going on. You turn your attention to helping reorder the discarded clothing.

After a few minutes, you glance up at the people coming through. You notice that they are spending much less time in the tent. People are taking the coat that's offered, and with a few exceptions where the size is wrong, they are leaving the tent with the first coat that they were given.

About half an hour later you step back outside to check the queue. To your surprise, only about ten people are left outside the tent. The sense of pushing and shoving has dropped right off. You turn to your colleague and ask what happened.

"I just told them they had a choice. Either they took the first coat they were offered, or else they would leave the tent empty-handed." She gives you the update with a smile, but there's no mistaking the firmness of the statement. You realise that on the receiving end of her instruction, you would have also complied.

You try to hide your surprise at how well she's calmed the whole situation down. You realise that her mix of kindness and strictness was just right for the situation. As you send her inside to get a break, you make a mental note to try to put her on crowd control for the tent in the nights to come.

Ends.

23

You think that your colleague's calming manner would be really helpful with the crowd, but you worry about sending her out alone in the current state of chaos. You decide to ask one of the male volunteers, a large young man, to work on crowd control. He agrees, then pulls on a raincoat and steps outside. You hear muffled sounds outside the tent, but you can't really tell what's going on. You turn your attention to helping reorder the discarded clothing.

After a few minutes, you glance up at the people coming through. You notice that they are behaving in quite a hostile manner. They snatch the coats that are offered, leaving very hastily.

About half an hour later you step back outside to check the queue. To your surprise, only about ten people are left outside the tent. The sense of pushing and shoving has dropped right off. You turn to your colleague and ask what happened.

"I devised my own system. I told them that there was a policeman sitting inside, behind the counter. When they got inside they had a choice. Either they took the first coat they were offered, or else they would be arrested and separated from their family. You have to be firm with these people, you know. That's what we learned in military service." He grins, seeming very pleased with his solution.

You try to hide your surprise at what he's done. His actions have certainly calmed the situation down, but the last thing you wanted was to associate your organisation and its assistance with the heavy-handed tactics of the local police.

As you send the volunteer inside to get a break, you make a mental note never to put him on crowd control for the tent again. **Ends.**

Personal values

An important starting point is to consider our own values. Do we even know them?

Some people hold a strong sense of value when it comes to issues of trust, honesty and reliability. Others have values which focus on helping the most vulnerable members of society. Some people are guided by the values of their religious beliefs, or by strong patterns of thought in their home country. Sometimes a life-changing circumstance, such as the loss of a loved one to a particular illness, leads to a value of compassion for others suffering a similar fate.

When looking at your own values, try to distinguish which are personal and cultural, and which are professional. Those coming from a medical background will be familiar with medical ethics, such as the need to allow a patient a level of choice in how much care they should receive. Following such values is different to following your cultural values; consider that in certain cultures, someone other than the patient decides what happens to them.

Before reading further, try to make a note of what you believe some of your values are in the box. To help get you started, some examples might include:

Fairness, honesty, care for those in need, hard work, equal distribution of wealth, equal choices for all people, freedom of speech.

Once you have your list, make a note by all of those which you think you might draw on when making decisions in disaster response. If possible, discuss them with a friend. This is best done with a friend from a culture different to your own.

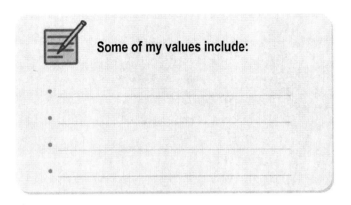

Some of my values include:

Ask them to draw up their own list, and compare the top five values you each have for life in general. Then consider what your top three values are in disaster response. How similar are these values across your two cultures?

Cultural values

Many disasters occur in cultures other than our own. One way to increase your ability to make good decisions when you are called to work in a different culture is to quickly build a basic understanding of values that are important in that location. If possible, do this with the help of a friend or colleague from the culture in question, and also by paying as much attention as you can to daily encounters between people.

Some things to observe or ask about include:

- The level of interaction between men and women; the level of physical contact between people.

- Behaviour that is taboo or causes offence, such as:

  Using the left hand for passing things; appropriate levels of clothing and how much uncovered skin is visible; smoking; drinking alcohol; pointing the soles of your feet at someone; pointing with your finger; touching someone's head; spitting; publicly blaming people; disagreeing with people.

A good starting point is to look at your own cultural taboos, to see how they compare with other people's.

Try to learn how to greet people in an appropriate manner, since this can give you a level of confidence when stepping into a tense or uncertain situation. Feeling comfortable in yourself is one thing; setting others at ease takes it even further. Just helping the people around you relax can put you on track to finding a favourable outcome in the situation.

By taking time to understand the values of the culture that you find yourself working in, you will find that some of your decisions make themselves. Try to be aware that where your own cultural values come into conflict with those of the place where you are working, you will generally be more effective in your decision making if you can give precedence to the host culture's values.

Humanitarian values

Disaster response can involve individuals and organisations from many different cultures and nations, all responding to the situation in ways that follow their own values. Given the range of often-conflicting personal and national values that exist, the potential for chaos is high. In order to create some level of consistent approach to helping people in need, many organisations look towards guiding principles such as the Red Cross Code of Conduct. [1]

A good starting point for new humanitarian workers is to look through the Code of Conduct, and take a moment to become familiar with its contents. Do you agree with all points? Are there points that you find hard to reconcile with your own values? Are there points which help you refine your values? Are there any values which you might not subscribe to in your daily life, but which you would be willing to follow specifically in a disaster response situation?

Those who have been active in disaster response for some time should take a moment to reflect on colleagues whose approaches you admired most. What values underlay their actions? What could you do to embed these values into your own approach? Sometimes just the act of reflecting on these values causes them to come to the surface and become a greater part of your own approach.

Being guided by our values

It's hard to know our own values without going through situations which cause us to reflect on them. When you read through the scenario for this chapter a second time, try to make a note of any values which come to mind at each decision point. Furthermore, try to distinguish between those which are your personal values, and those which you apply more from a professional viewpoint.

Even applying a professional viewpoint can bring us into situations of conflict: In the first of the scenarios, which is more important? To support the concept of treating people with dignity – which was shown by the choice to give good quality headscarves? Or to support the greatest number of people possible – which was the choice to buy as many scarves as possible?

The first option fits well with Point Eight in the Code of Conduct, which focuses on reducing future vulnerabilities. As a result of being treated well, the lady whose sense of dignity was addressed was in a better place to treat her children well. By focusing on strengthening the mother, relief efforts would have an impact on her entire family. The knock-on effects of this could be significant.

Yet the alternative option fits well with Point Two in the Code of Conduct, which notes that aid priorities are calculated on the basis of needs alone, without adverse distinction of any kind. In this case the needs of those who came after the first beneficiaries were equally important, and should not be outranked by the needs of a select few to feel more special.

Many situations that you will encounter in disaster response will not have a clear precedent for how to respond. As mentioned before, there is often no 'right' answer. In trying to respond, it is your own values that will drive your decisions. In such situations, it's important to know your values. As one author on the subject of ethics, Stephen Adeney, has noted,

At the point where we have to make a decision, we are unlikely to reflect on [what is] more appropriate. The kind of person we are and the way that we are orientated to God, to our neighbour and to our own self-interest will most likely decide for us. [2]

The moral choices that you make in disaster response may bring you into conflict with others. Knowing your own values helps you express more clearly to others why you are following a particular course of action. And knowing the generally accepted values of humanitarian aid helps you measure if your responses are in line with what many others would also wish to do.

When to put aside our own values

Clearly there are times when there is a need to apply judgement based on your own values, such as in the case of the headscarves. The decision maker's cultural background, gender, personality and motivations will all play a role in the final decision.

But there are times when applying your own values may be a self-indulgence which should be kept out of disaster response. Sometimes when dealing with overwhelming humanitarian needs your values have to be put aside. In the case of giving sugar to a mother for her baby's bottle, your own cultural values may scream out at you that this is not okay. But is it your right to impose that on a mother trying to keep her baby alive through the night, giving it the small level of comfort it is used to? If the baby refuses to drink unsweetened milk and develops hypothermia as a result, is that a better outcome?

The warning for those making decisions is to be very careful of value judgements that relate to a culturally acceptable way of doing things. This can include decisions involving the roles of men, women and children in society; the use of cigarettes, alcohol, caffeine or junk food; the approach to safety in vehicles and in other situations; the distribution of food between family members; the use of outright lying to get a desired result; or other decision points relating to cultural values.

Balancing conflicting values

In order to make effective decisions that others can support and follow, it is important to realise that moving across the world to help with a situation of disaster does not give you the right to impose your own values on the groups that you are helping. Adeney's suggestion is that, in cross-cultural encounters where situations of value conflict cannot be avoided, it becomes essential "to know how to choose higher values over lesser values." [3]

Developing this ability to distinguish between conflicting values in decision making is essential. As you read through the subsequent scenarios in this book, try to note any time a value conflict comes into your response. Take the opportunity to discover which values are guiding your response. Are the prevailing values in your responses the ones which really mean the most to you? Or do you need to adjust your hierarchy of values in order to be more effective in high-pressure, cross-cultural situations? Rather than expecting others to be guided by your values, try to distinguish between your own higher and lower values, and be careful to limit the weight that you give to your lower, culturally-specific values.

In addition, working in a team in disaster response, with colleagues from a number of different backgrounds, will inevitably lead to an added level of strain in some decision points. Some methods for understanding and managing these conflicts will be covered in chapters four and seven.

You can develop a level of expertise in decision making by forcing yourself to wrestle with conflicting values, well ahead of any actual encounter. Choosing to think through situations in advance means that when a decision point is encountered in reality, you will have already developed an appropriate response to the conflict of values. At this point you will be able to perceive the conflict for what it is, rather than be immobilised by it. The thinking that you have done in advance will direct your response, making it seem instinctive or spontaneous.

It has been suggested that this type of 'spontaneous' response is not random, but rather the result of underlying structure created by the decision maker [4]. By working through questions of value conflict in your mind well ahead of any encounter with a flashpoint, you will soon begin to develop 'the structure for spontaneity.' [5]

Values:

Principles to remember

CHAPTER THREE

COMPROMISE

Facing a request for assistance is a very common theme in disaster response. In addition to the aid beneficiaries whom your organisation is focused on serving, there is the more subtle challenge of requests for help from individuals or groups *around* the disaster environment.

Developing proactive strategies for responding to these requests can help you to make many decisions more quickly and with more confidence.

Scenario Three

After your successes delivering food aid to people displaced by the fighting (Scenario One), your agency has asked you to take the lead on a series of medical distributions.

From your base in the city you've been reaching out to several more isolated towns. You were nervous at first, given the number of different groups operating in the area, and their ever-shifting loyalties. Going to all these remote towns was quite different to the simple food run you had been making. But you soon realised that your efforts were respected by the different groups you met.

Your normal refrigerated truck has been having mechanical problems, and you've been forced to ask around to find a vehicle suitable to keep your supplies of medicine at the best temperature. You've found a temporary solution, an older Land Cruiser with a partially working air conditioner. The cooling unit can't really keep up with the relentless daytime heat, but you've been able to scrape together a number of chiller boxes and some ice packs.

You calculate that you have about three hours before the contents start to be affected by the heat. The town that you are headed towards takes approximately that long to get to. You realise that the medicines will be okay as long as the town's clinic has their fridges waiting with space prepared.

Taking a team of four others with you, you leave your base and set off for the distant town.

The first part of the journey passes without incident. Then, about an hour away from the town, you reach a checkpoint. It's mid-afternoon, and a number of armed men sprawl around on old chairs under a huge mango tree. A lot of empty beer cans lie on the floor.

You pull to a halt in front of the dented pole that serves as a barrier. The mango tree is so vast that the whole checkpoint is under its shade. The soldier at the checkpoint asks for your vehicle papers and your ID. After glancing through them carefully for a few minutes he points out a spelling mistake on the name of your vehicle on the paperwork. You hadn't paid much attention to this paperwork when you borrowed the vehicle, assuming that everything was in order since the vehicle was in regular use.

Do you return to the city to get the paperwork fixed?

Yes: go to 1

Otherwise go to 3

1 You turn to the others. "I think we'd better return. We don't want this kind of problem at other checkpoints."

But your colleague doesn't agree. "I'm not sure that's the best thing to do," she says. "I don't think another two hours of the heat will be good for the medicine. Also, we've been stopped on different occasions and there's always a way through. Can't we see what we can do to keep going?"

Do you want to see if there is a way to proceed?

Yes: go to 3

Otherwise go to 2

2 "No," you say. I just don't think we can take the chance. We'd better go back. The medicines should be okay a bit longer than we planned."

"Can we at least ring the hospital and check what they want us to do?" your colleague asks.

Explaining to the soldier that you need to make a call, you open the antenna of the satellite phone and make a call. You're pleased that the director answers quickly, and you explain the situation to her. After listening to you, she asks to be put on the phone with the soldier at the checkpoint.

After listening for a couple of minutes, the soldier offers a few quick replies. You watch his body language. He seems quite relaxed as he chats. Then he hands the phone back to you.

"It's okay." The hospital director's voice is faint on the phone. You try to block out the sounds of the soldiers joking beside the tree. "He says he can help you with the paperwork. They know the clinic you're going to. They understand why they should help."

Relieved, you end the call and put the phone back in the glove box, then turn to get your paperwork back from the soldier.

Go to 3

3 "It's fine," the soldier says, "A simple mistake. We can see that you've got important goods on board. We don't want to hold you up. It would take our boss two hours to get here and give you a cover letter for the mistake. So we'll help you out and let you keep going."

You're pleased that the situation has resolved itself. As you start to thank him, he continues: "Since we're helping you, you can help us out too. These two soldiers need to get back to our base near the town you're going to. You can give them a lift in the back of your truck."

As you start to discuss amongst your team, the two soldiers come up. They smell faintly of alcohol, and you don't like the sleazy look one of them gives one of your team mates.

One of your team members doesn't want to take the soldiers. "It's very lonely out there on the road; they could start trouble and no-one would be able to help us," he whispers. "Besides, doesn't one of our agency rules say that we can't take weapons on our vehicle? Those guys each have a rifle."

Your second team mate feels very differently. "There are reports of bandits on this road, and they often seem to target aid vehicles. If we have these soldiers on board, I know they won't attack us. Someone at the meeting last week was talking about how well it went for them when they used an armed guard."

Your third team mate seems uncertain. "I agree about the safety against bandits," she explains. "I'm actually very nervous about a bandit attack. But I'm also really worried about the people in the places we're going to. Weren't they attacked by soldiers from this group a few months ago, before the truce? What are they going to think if they see us associated with the soldiers? Do you think we'll be able to explain why they are with us? Our language skills aren't great."

Do you agree to give the soldiers a lift?

Yes: go to 4

Maybe: go to 5

Otherwise go to 8

4 You decide that the medicines are a priority, and that the threat of banditry is a compelling reason to take advantage of an armed escort. You decide to compromise against the risk of how you are perceived by getting the soldier to agree with his men that they must leave the vehicle at a checkpoint five miles out of town, where your maps shows a small military outpost.

You rearrange the team so that the soldiers are in the front row of the truck cab, with the female team members on the rear row, out of normal vision. Then you start on your way.

Within ten minutes of driving, one of the soldiers starts making suggestive comments towards your passengers. You find yourself getting very uncomfortable. This continues for several minutes, and then the man falls asleep.

In a small roadside village, rough mounds in the dirt road act to slow passing vehicles. As you drive along at a reduced pace, your gaze turns to several villagers as they walk along the road. You are quite surprised at the hard glares coming at your vehicle. You've always found people in these roadside villages to be fairly friendly in the past.

You reach a dried-up riverbed. The road twists down and bumps across the parched ground. At the bumping the soldiers wake up and look around for their bearings. As you pull up from the riverbed on the far side they tell you to let them off the vehicle. They thank you and start walking in the direction of a small military base that is visible off in the distance.

Go to 9

5 You know that your agency is firm on the "no weapons" policy.

Do you offer the soldiers a lift if they leave their weapons behind?

Yes: go to 7

Maybe: go to 6

Otherwise: go to 8

6 You realise that you can make a couple of spaces between the medicine boxes in the rear, where the soldiers will be almost out of sight.

Knowing this, do you offer a lift if the weapons are left behind?

Yes: go to 7

Otherwise: go to 8

7

You explain to the group of soldiers that your agency policy does not allow you to take weapons on board the vehicle.

One of the men who wants a lift speaks up. "We can leave our weapons," he says. "They can bring them to us tomorrow. But we really need to get to base to go to a clinic."

You rearrange the team so that the soldiers are seated low among the chiller boxes in the rear of the vehicle, out of normal vision. Then you start on your way.

Within ten minutes of driving both soldiers fall fast asleep. You pass another checkpoint, but when the soldier operating the pole barrier sees the two uniformed men in the back he waves you through. You're starting to get worried about the medicines, so you're very glad to avoid any more questions about the Land Cruiser's paperwork.

In a small roadside village, rough mounds in the dirt road act to slow passing vehicles. As you drive along at a reduced pace, your gaze turns to several villagers as they walk along the road. You find yourself responding instinctively to their friendly waves. You remind yourself how important it is that your agency keeps helping people such as this, despite the pressures of the conflict.

After more driving you reach a dried-up riverbed. The road twists down and bumps across the parched ground. At the bumping the soldiers wake up and look around for their bearings. As you pull up from the riverbed on the far side they tell you to let them off the vehicle. They thank you and start walking in the direction of a small military base that is visible off in the distance.

Go to 9

8 You explain to the soldier that your agency policy does not allow you to take weapons on board the vehicle. Also, to support your case, you point to the limited seating in the truck.

The soldier on the checkpoint gets quite upset. "It looks like we might have an issue with your paperwork after all," he growls.

Then one soldier speaks up. "I can leave my rifle," he says. "They can bring it to me tomorrow. But I really need to get to the base to go to a clinic."

You briefly confer with your team and decide that you are safer if only one soldier goes with you, and if he is unarmed. Also, you are starting to get very concerned about how long the medicine will remain cool.

You agree to let one, unarmed soldier join you, and quickly continue on your way.

When you are 30 minutes away from the town, the soldier tells you to let him off the truck. He thanks you and walks away in the direction of a small military base in the distance.

Go to 9

9 The road enters a thick band of forest. Looking at the map you printed out earlier, you judge that you must be quite close to the town now, no more than about 15 minutes away. You drive around a tight bend in the road, and suddenly find yourself facing another checkpoint. By now you're concerned for the state of the medicine and want to get it into the clinic's cold store without any further delay.

At this checkpoint the soldiers wear different, older uniforms. Despite the warmth, their faces are obscured by balaclavas, only their eyes and mouths remaining visible. As you look into their eyes when you stop the vehicle, you sense a real coldness.

One soldier leans in through your open window. "I see you're bringing medicine," he says. "It's good that you want to help these people. But my men need medicine too."

You start to explain that the clinic makes all the decisions about who gets the medicine.

"No," he says, bringing his gun up into sight. "I decide."

He gives you a choice. Either they take as much medicine as they need, and you can carry on and take the rest to the clinic. Or you can turn your truck around and return to the city.

One of your team members insists that you should give him some medicine. "We're so close," he explains, "at least the clinic will get most of what they need. It will save lives. Otherwise it will all be ruined."

Another team member is really opposed. "We were warned about this group in a security briefing," she says. "They've committed horrible crimes on the people of these villages. If we help their health, we're just assisting them to commit more crimes. If they stay sick, they can't harm the people of the villages anymore."

The third member of your team is a nurse. "When we trained," she explains, "we were taught to give assistance based on need, not on our judgement of the person. If these soldiers are sick and need some medicine, we have an obligation to help."

The rest of the team turn to you. "We can't agree," they say. "You choose for us."

Do you agree to let him take some of the medicine?

Yes: go to 10

Maybe: go to 11

Otherwise go to 13

10

You consider your colleague's point that you should help all who are sick with the medicine, without judgement.

You also consider the effect of turning around – all the medicine would spoil in the heat, and in addition the town's supply won't be replenished.

You decide that even if the soldiers take half your medicine, at least you will have something for the town clinic.

You agree to let the soldiers take some medicine, but do your best negotiating to limit the amount they take. To your surprise, they only want four boxes. You realise that you can give the boxes which are most likely to be heat-damaged, keeping the best-quality items for the town clinic.

As soon as the soldiers have the four boxes, you drive on and soon reach the town clinic.

Accompanied by the clinic staff, you and your team rapidly unload the boxes. To your relief, all the medicine contained in the boxes is in good condition.

You mention your encounter to the clinic manager. He describes another road out of town, one that skirts the edge of the forest. He assures you that if you return that way you'll avoid the forest checkpoint. You thank him for his advice and prepare for the journey back.

Ends.

11 You decide to try negotiating to limit the amount that the soldiers take. To your surprise, they only want four small boxes. You realise that you can give the boxes which are most likely to be heat-damaged, keeping the best-quality items for the town clinic.

You also consider the effect of turning around – all the medicine would spoil in the heat, and in addition the town's supply won't be replenished.

You conclude that four boxes is a very small amount compared with the benefit that you'll bring to the clinic. You instruct your colleague to pick four boxes from the supply at the back. You quietly tell them to make sure they pick the most heat-affected ones.

As soon as the soldiers have the four boxes, the man on the barrier raises the pole and beckons you through. You drive on quickly, very aware of the amount of time you've spent at the different stops.

You soon reach the town clinic. Accompanied by the clinic staff, you and your team rapidly unload the boxes. To your relief, all the medicine contained in the boxes is in good condition. You mention your encounter to the clinic manager. He describes another road out of town, one that skirts the edge of the forest. He assures you that if you return that way you'll avoid the forest checkpoint. You thank him for his advice and prepare for the journey back.

Ends.

12 You realise that no matter how you look at the situation, and no matter what other agencies do, you can't be part of helping those who are responsible for the conflict.

You decide to return to your main base, and hope that some of the medicine will still be useful elsewhere, even if some is heat-damaged.

Two of your colleagues object strongly. They really want to push through. You explain firmly that you've been asked to lead the work, and that in this type of situation they're required to follow your decisions. You spend the first half hour in a heated discussion. They finally go quiet, but the long drive home is mainly filled with a sullen silence.

Ends.

13

You decide that you simply cannot help the soldiers who regularly attack the local civilians, even if this action also prevents the town's clinic receiving medicine.

You decide to return to your main base, and hope that some of the medicine will still be useful elsewhere, even if some is heat-damaged.

As you're preparing to turn around, another large four-wheel drive vehicle pulls up beside you. You recognise the agency logos which are plastered on the bonnet and side doors. The group are well known in the NGO community for having an effective operation.

The soldier from the checkpoint walks over to the new vehicle. You watch as the passenger gets out, walks to the back of the vehicle and pulls out two medium-sized cardboard boxes. He stacks one on top of the other, adjusts his balance and carries them towards the soldier.

The soldier points to some bare ground beside the barrier pole. While the passenger sets down the boxes, the soldier raises the barrier and waves the new vehicle through.

"It looks like they're okay with it," one of your teammates mutters. "Shouldn't we do the same?"

Do you reconsider your approach and allow the soldiers to take some medicine?

Yes: go to 11

Otherwise go to 12

Compromise

It may help to consider that almost all disaster response involves some form of compromise.

For example, there is usually compromise between which activity to focus funds on. Once an organisation has the results of a thorough needs assessment, conflicting priorities will often emerge. Good project managers will take into account a number of factors – such as community requests, the organisation's specialities, the feasibility of the project, potential other agencies nearby and so on – when deciding where to prioritise.

A starting point for effective decision making under pressure is to become comfortable with an environment of compromise, the way a champion athlete becomes accustomed to an environment of discomfort. It's simply part of the reality. The alternative is to carry a very black-and-white outlook into situations which often have no clear 'right' outcome.

Prioritising objectives

Becoming comfortable with compromise doesn't mean ignoring good guidelines or legal principles. It doesn't mean taking an 'anything goes' attitude to relief work. But it means identifying the overall goal very clearly. And then from this, developing strategies, ideally in advance, that will allow you to achieve the overall goal.

In the process of identifying these overall goals, a 'priority of objectives' will begin to emerge. From this priority it will be possible to identify points which might need to be compromised on, and points which are the very last things to be compromised on.

In this chapter's scenario, there is a clear overall goal:

- Get medicines to people who require them. This is the agency's reason for being there.

There are also sub-objectives:

- Do not support or empower the group(s) who are harming the target group.
- Do not undertake activities that make it harder for the team and other groups to work in the future.
- Do not expose staff to unnecessary levels of risk.

Using this list, an agency can develop a series of positions to take:

Ideal position: We will deliver all the medicine only to the most needy recipients, while keeping our staff completely free from risk and while not contributing anything to the overall situation of harm faced by the recipients. We will strictly adhere to national and international laws and we will ensure that our work builds a supportive environment for other aid agencies, be they national or international.

At the other extreme, the agency may choose:

Worst case: We will deliver some of the medicine to some of the recipients. However, we will allow our staff to be exposed to significant risk and contribute significantly to the overall situation of harm faced by the recipients. We will ignore all national and international laws and we will completely disregard the effect of our actions on other aid agencies, be they national or international.

Many agencies would find the 'worst case' unacceptable. In circumstances which forced them to only work in such a manner, they would most likely suspend programming.

However, the reality is that many agencies operate in conditions which are less than the 'ideal' approach, with significant success.

Based on this observation, it seems reasonable to conclude that agencies accept a certain amount of compromise in order to achieve their goals. For the front-line decision maker, it can be very helpful to start to learn these points of compromise, the amount of compromise on each point, and most importantly, which ones are 'deal-breakers.'

To simplify things at this stage it is assumed that the individual decision maker and the organisation that they work for are in complete agreement about everything. This is rarely the case, and the subject of conflicting approaches is considered more in the next chapter. But at this point, no distinction is made between the individual and the agency.

Developing experience with compromise

One aspect of 'experience' that can be built up quickly is an understanding of how much compromise is permissible on a particular issue. Looking back at some of the decision points in the simulation, there were issues of:

- Providing a level of aid to those in need
- Carrying members of the armed forces / militia
- Carrying people under the influence of alcohol / drugs
- Carrying weapons on the vehicle
- Supporting people who are harming those you are serving

As discussed, the overall reason for being there was to bring medicine to people who needed it. If, for example, all the medicine was taken at a checkpoint, does this then mean there is no point carrying on?

Not necessarily. What if simply being an international presence in the affected town helps reduce incidents of violence? What if arriving in the town with a vehicle becomes a means of evacuation of very sick patients? Even the main goal should be carefully examined, to see if there is more to it underneath the surface.

The scenario brought up other issues. These included:

1. Supporting the people who are causing the harm.

A number of factors are at work here. In many cases, especially where militia are involved, some members may in part be victims themselves, conscripted from the populations you are there to help, and forced to serve against their will. Their need for support may be as genuine as the end recipients.

In other cases, such as where cycles of revenge are occurring, it can be hard to define who is the aggressor and who is the victim. A group of aggressors may still be suffering from the attacks which were carried out on them in recent times.

Another question to consider is if the conflict will continue regardless of whether you help the aggressor group or not. If it is likely to continue regardless, you may decide that by supporting the aggressor group, you at least gain freedom to support the most needy in the town. This in turn may be the best chance that those patients have of recovering sufficiently in order to flee future attacks.

2. Carrying members of the armed forces / militia.

   In addition to the risk of being perceived as endorsing a particular military group, carrying soldiers in an agency vehicle may be portrayed as making the vehicle a target for opposition forces. However, sometimes this can be helpful. In areas known for banditry, the presence of a soldier may well reduce overall exposure to risk, for bandits will be more reluctant to attack. Furthermore, where multiple road blocks by the same armed force exist, carrying a member of the armed group can speed your passage through subsequent roadblocks.

   In addition to developing judgement skills which take these questions into account, you will have to familiarise yourself with the specifics of the conflict in your particular situation. An approach which is suitable in one location may be less suitable in a different conflict.

3. Carrying people under the influence of substances.

   What is your initial impression of their state? Are they 'wired' or are they sleepy? What is the composition of your team? Do you have individuals with the maturity to handle an unruly passenger? A sleepy, unarmed drunk, resting between two competent staff members on a hot afternoon presents a different risk from a 'wired', talkative, argumentative passenger in a vehicle full of inexperienced new staff.

4. Carrying weapons on the vehicle.

   In a high-profile area the vehicle may have a "No Weapons" sticker. This can help overcome language barriers when explaining that weapons can't be carried. But weapons can also introduce a good compromise point. For example, you may be able to compromise with the suggestion that "Yes we will take the individual requiring a lift, but we cannot bring their weapon on board."

Actively seeking compromise points

If you start from the premise that disaster response is a compromise, then you can actively look for compromise points. Rather than confront a request from a person in a position of power with a straight "No", you can show your willingness to help *to a certain point.* "No" becomes "Yes, we would like to help, but we can only help up to this certain point." In many cultures it is common that a request is not expected to be met in full. By showing that you are willing to work towards accommodating a request, you give yourself a stronger basis for sticking to the items that you really can't compromise on.

Effective decision making in disaster response is supported by knowing what your goals are, and which objectives you are able to compromise on, and to what degree. Working through these questions, in advance, can help you approach decision situations as points for *acceptable compromise*, rather than as sticking points.

Before you return to the scenario a second time, think about what you are going to encounter and take a moment to list your own priority of objectives. Try to identify your main priorities and your sub-priorities. Which of your sub-priorities can you easily compromise on? Which could you compromise on as a last resort? Which of them are you unwilling to compromise on?

Additionally, thinking back to the previous chapter, which of these decisions are being driven by your own values? Which are being driven by the generally accepted values of humanitarian response? Are there situations where you need to use your judgement to go against these general values, in light of a specific case?

Once you have these values, priorities and possible compromise points in mind, return to the scenario. Try to see each decision point in light of these priorities.

Compromise:

Principles to remember

CHAPTER FOUR

GIFTS, BRIBES
& EXTORTION

Many aspects of disaster response involve the transfer of resources. It may be cash or vouchers, or it may be physical goods. In this environment of resource transfer, it is inevitable that requests by people other than the direct beneficiaries will occur. If you respond to these requests, are you giving a gift, paying a bribe, or responding to extortion? Knowing how to make a distinction between different requests can speed up the decision-making process significantly.

Furthermore, it's one thing to face a challenging situation by yourself. Having evaluated your main objectives, you may know your compromise points. But what if you're joined by colleagues with different views? Or what if your approach is at odds with that of your organisation? This chapter also looks at decision making when different viewpoints are actively involved.

Scenario Four

As far as donors go, you feel your organisation is fairly lucky. Some of its biggest donors are retired aid workers, and they generally avoid tying staff up with long proposals and project reports. But they do insist on seeing each crisis first hand.

Your team is very busy, but you really value these donors, and the experience and insights that they bring. You agreed to host a group of three of them for a week.

They've been here for two days, and yesterday they were able to go out to a food distribution in the neighbouring town. Today is quieter, and you've sent your senior administrator, Casandra, with them on a driving tour of the city. Casandra is just back to part-time work after her maternity leave, and as is the practice in the culture she has her baby, Innocence, with her. You decided that a gentle drive around the city, with a stop at the well-known cliff look-out above the river, would be a relaxing task for her.

You're getting through some emails which have piled up while you've been hosting the visitors.

Your phone rings.

"Hi Casandra, are you finished already?"

"What? No. Listen, I don't know what to do! He wants me to go with him, but he won't let me bring Innocence with me! And Doug doesn't have his inhaler. What are we going to do?"

Confused, you ask her to explain what she means.

"It's this policeman. He stopped me. He said I didn't indicate, but I know I did. I'm always so careful when I have my children with me. He says I have to come to the police station and pay the fine. But he won't let me take my baby. And all these guests have to stay with the car as well. And Doug's really worried. He thinks he left his inhaler in the office this morning after the security briefing."

You glance around the office. Sure enough, on top of the small office fridge is the distinctive blue inhaler.

"But listen," Casandra continues. "He says it's easier if I just pay the fine here. I can just keep going and he'll write up the ticket when he gets back to the office. But I know he'll just put the money in his own pocket. What should I do?"

Do you advise her to pay the fine?

Yes: go to 1

Maybe: 2

Otherwise go to 3

1 Just pay him the fine, you tell Casandra.

"Alright, if you think that's okay. Then I'm coming right back."

Half an hour later you hear the car pull in. Glancing out of the office window you see two of the visitors walking up towards the accommodation block.

The office door opens and Casandra comes in, carrying Innocence in a baby capsule. Doug is right behind her. He spots his inhaler on the fridge and grabs it with a sheepish look.

"Beginner's mistake. I should have known better. I'm really sorry for the trouble I caused."

You're more concerned about Casandra. She looks really upset. After setting the baby capsule down under her desk she collapses into her chair.

"You know, our mayor is campaigning so hard against corruption. All the business people are getting behind it. And now I've gone and made things worse by paying to get away from a problem. But I know for sure I didn't drive wrong."

She opens her desk drawer and pulls out a folder. "So how do I record this in my petty cash?"

Do you insist that she pays the fine from her personal money?

Yes: go to 7
Maybe: go to 8
Otherwise go to 9

2 You know that sometimes asking for a receipt helps distinguish between a genuine request and one that is for personal gain. You wonder if asking for a receipt as she makes payment will help Casandra avoid a corrupt situation.

Do you suggest that she pays the fine and asks for a receipt?

Yes: Go to 4

Otherwise go to 3

3 You remember a situation in the past where someone else was able to go to pay a traffic fine on behalf of a busy staff member.

You know roughly where she is. It's about a thirty minute drive from the office.

Do you tell Casandra to ask the policemen if someone can drive out to her, and go to pay the fine on her behalf?

Yes: go to 5

Otherwise go to 6

4
You suggest that she pays and asks for a receipt.

She keeps the phone on, and you hear her in discussion with the policeman. It becomes clear that there won't be a receipt if she pays on the spot.

Do you advise her to pay?

Yes: go to 1

Otherwise go to 3

5
Casandra agrees.

"I know it is a big inconvenience for them. But I really can't leave Innocence. And Doug is getting very worried about his asthma now, with all this dust. I'll just check with the policeman."

You hear her faintly in the background, as she talks with the policeman.
A moment later her voice is clear in the speaker again.

"He says we can't do that. Either I pay him the fine now, or I have to leave Innocence and go with him. I can't do that."

Do you advise her to pay the fine?

Yes: go to 1

Otherwise go to 6

6

You hear a new male voice in the background. The voices are faint, and you can't make out what's being said.

A few moments later Casandra's voice comes through clearly again.

"That was Doug. He paid the fine. He told me we had to keep moving, so he could get his inhaler. I'm not sure he should have done that, but he looks really worried. Anyway, I'm driving back now. See you soon."

Half an hour later you hear the car pull in. Glancing out of the office window you see two of the visitors walking up towards the accommodation block.

The office door opens and Casandra comes in, carrying Innocence in a baby capsule. Doug is right behind her. He spots his inhaler on the fridge and grabs it with a sheepish look.

"Beginner's mistake. I should have known better. I'm really sorry for the trouble I caused."

You're more concerned about Casandra. She looks really upset. After setting the baby capsule down under her desk she collapses into her chair.

"You know, our mayor is campaigning so hard against corruption. All the business people are getting behind it. And now I've gone and made things worse by paying to get away from a problem. But I know for sure I didn't drive wrong."

She opens her desk drawer and pulls out a folder. "I paid Doug back from my cash float. He didn't want to take the money but I was driving, I was the one stopped. Anyway, how do I record the payment in my petty cash?"

Do you insist that she pays the fine from her personal money?

Yes: 7

Maybe: 8

Otherwise go to 9

7 You explain to Casandra that as the driver, she's responsible for paying any fine from when she was driving.

She seems really surprised.

"I thought I'd get a bit more support than this. I don't think I want to help as a driver again if it turns out this way. Next time please ask someone else to do the driving."

She turns away in her chair, then suddenly swivels back to face you.

"You know, I'm really surprised at you. I thought you understood the pressures here. Now I realise, you don't understand at all."

Go to 13

8 You inform Casandra that she can record the fine as a transport cost, and write up a receipt for it which you will sign for her.

Or, if she prefers, she can pay the fine from her own money. After thinking about it for a moment, she asks if she can write it as a transport expense. You agree, and sign the small receipt voucher she passes to you.

As you do so, you remind yourself how different things are here.

Go to 12

9 You feel it's important that she understands the difference between a forced payment, and one that's made to get a special favour. But you know from experience that's a long discussion.

Do you take the time to explain the situation to her?

Yes: go to 10

Otherwise go to 11

10

You take some time to go through an explanation with Casandra. You help her understand that by threatening to take her away from her baby, the policeman was introducing a physical and psychological threat. You also explain that the situation was made more urgent due to the potential health risk to Doug.

After a while you see her relax again. You ask her to fill out a receipt voucher for the cost of the fine. As you sign the receipt, you remind yourself how different things are here. You are pleased to think that many of your donors, like the group currently visiting, understand the pressures of running relief projects in these conditions.

You make a mental note to chat with the donors about it later in the day, to make sure they were all clear on what happened.
Go to 12

11

You inform Casandra that she can record the fine as a transport cost, and write up a receipt for it which you will sign for her.

A few minutes later she brings you a small receipt voucher to sign. As you sign the receipt, you remind yourself how different things are here. You are pleased to think that many of your donors, like the group currently visiting, understand the pressures of running relief projects in these conditions.

You make a mental note to chat with the donors about it later in the day, to make sure they were all clear on what happened.
Go to 12

12

You decided last night that you would send the donors out to one of the remotest towns, where your distributions are really having an impact. To get there means travelling by chartered light aircraft, for the roads leading to the town are far too insecure for travel by car. You have been supplying so many goods that you currently have an aircraft chartered for every Tuesday morning. You also appreciate the chance to get a full day's work done without having to host the donors.

You always split the charter with another agency, to save on your overall costs. They use the aircraft on its journey from the capital to your city, and then you use the onward flight to move your goods. To give the greatest payload possible out of the capital, the aircraft charter company has asked you to stock drums of fuel at your compound. Each week they refuel two drums' worth of fuel when they load your goods.

Soon after breakfast you all crowd into your pickup truck, which has two drums of fuel strapped down in the back. Your colleague follows with a truck loaded with food packs and mosquito nets. After dropping the donors at the passenger terminal to have their documents checked, you drive around to the tarmac where the aircraft is parked. The guard at the airport gate recognises your vehicles and waves you through.

While your colleague works with the pilot to load the goods into the plane, you back the pickup truck under the wing, attach the fuel pump to one of the drums, and start refueling the plane. The drum is soon empty, and you start on the second.

You hear a voice call out. One of the aircraft marshallers is standing below you, leaning on the pickup door. Over the noise of the other aircraft, he calls out that he would like the empty drum when you're finished with it.

You have got quite used to all the different requests for things. One long-established colleague warned you recently that it's a slippery slope - as soon as people see you helping one person, they all want something. They advised you to be really careful when the demands for goods start to flow. They also explained the cost involved. You know, for example, that a good fuel drum can fetch quite a price in the local market.

You know from recent experience that the marshaller can have quite an important role in getting your aircraft away on time. If he chooses to give other planes priority it can add up to half an hour to the plane's departure. You know that the pilot has a long route to fly that day and is keen to keep moving.

Do you allow the marshaller to take the empty drum?

Yes: go to 14   Maybe: go to 13

Otherwise go to 16

13   You want the marshaller's help but you don't want to give the impression that you are happy to just give things away.

Do you offer to sell him the drum?

Yes: go to 15   Otherwise go to 16

14 You decide that it's important to keep the marshaller happy. You pass down the empty drum. He takes it, lies it down, and starts rolling it towards his small equipment cabin. You notice a few other drums stacked up there.

The aircraft leaves without incident, and you're soon back at your base. As you park the pickup truck your colleague walks past.

"Where's the second drum?" he asks. You explain what happened.

"Oh, you've got to be kidding me. Don't you see what you've done? They'll be all over us next time for more drums. And not just drums. Food donations, buckets, all sorts. Didn't you hear what I explained the other day?"

You try to explain that you wanted to keep the plane moving.

"You don't get it, do you? It's not the marshaller who decides who has priority. It's the control tower. I knew I should have gone myself." He pauses for a minute, and calms down.

"Look, I suppose it's not your fault. You're not used to dealing with these guys. But you've got to be strategic. You can't just go giving away things to everyone you meet. If you're going to do it, make sure you get the top guys. They'll bring everyone else into line. Now I'd better let the others know, so they can expect fresh demands the next time they go there."

He walks away towards the lunch room.
Go to 26

15

Knowing what the drums cost in the market, you call out a price to the marshaller. He asks if he can pay slightly less, and you agree. You pass down the empty drum. He takes it, lies it down, and starts rolling it towards his small equipment cabin. You notice a few other drums stacked up there.

The aircraft leaves without incident, and you're soon back at your base. As you park the truck your colleague walks past.

"Where's the second drum?" he asks. You explain what happened.

"Oh, you've got to be kidding me. Don't you see what you've done? They'll be all over us next time for more drums. And not just drums. Food donations, buckets, all sorts. Didn't you hear what I explained the other day?"

You try to explain that you wanted to keep the plane moving.

"You don't get it, do you? It's not the marshaller who decides who has priority. It's the control tower. I knew I should have gone myself." He pauses for a minute, and calms down.

"Look, I suppose it's not your fault. You're not used to dealing with these guys. But you've got to be strategic. You can't just go helping out everyone you meet. If you're going to do it, make sure you get the top guys. They'll bring everyone else into line. Now I'd better let the others know, so they can expect fresh demands the next time they go there."

He walks away towards the lunch room.

Go to 26

16

Mindful of your colleague's advice, you tell the marshaller you're not able to give him the drum. You explain that you need it to be filled and used again when the next plane comes in.

The pilot calls out to you that they're in a hurry and need to keep moving. Yet the marshaller appears in no rush at all and is still leaning on the pickup door.

You remember that you carry sets of earplugs in the pickup's glovebox. Your colleague said he sometimes gives them out at the airport because it bothers him that people work around such noisy planes without any ear protection. You're not sure if the earplugs are reserved for particular people or if you can just give them out.

Do you offer the marshaller a set of earplugs?

Yes: go to 17

Otherwise go to 18

17

The marshaller takes the earplugs that you offer. He seems very pleased.

As soon as the pilot has closed up the aircraft and started the engine, the marshaller beckons him forward.

You drive towards the control tower to file the pilot's paperwork.

Go to 19

18

You tell the marshaller that you don't have anything you can give him.

He casts a gaze at the back of the plane, where all the goods are loaded. Then he walks away down the tarmac.

"Where's he going?" the pilot asks. "We need him to bring us out. Now I suppose we'll have to wait until he's finished with that other plane up there. What a waste of time."

Go to 19

19

You walk up the winding steps that lead to the top of the control tower. The view is expansive, the windows giving a three hundred and sixty degree view around the airfield. The cool breeze flowing through the open windows is a welcome relief after the effort of climbing all the stairs.

You recognise the air traffic controller from an earlier visit. He doesn't use your name, but welcomes you openly, and asks for the flight plan.

"By the way," he says as he takes the plan from you, "I saw you refuelling down there. You know, I really need a drum for my house. I want to collect the rainwater from my roof so it doesn't all go to waste. It's better for my children to drink than this tap water."

You recall your earlier conversation with your colleague. They had mentioned that everyone who wants something has a convincing story of need. But many of them are often untrue. They told you it's almost impossible to judge based on a story.

Do you refuse him bluntly, so that he knows not to ask again next time?

Yes: go to 20

Otherwise go to 21

20 You are quite abrupt, telling him there are no drums available for anyone. For a moment he seems taken aback by your reply. Then he turns to the flight plan.

"Look, the pilot hasn't signed in the box. I can't file this."

You look at where he is pointing. A small part of the pilot's scribbled signature has gone outside of the signature box. You know that it's nothing. But, unfortunately, you know that the controller has the authority to release or hold planes on the tarmac.

"You'll need to get him to fill out a new one. Bring it back when you're done."

As you head down the steps you know the pilot is going to be really upset. The extra paperwork and the delay in submission will easily add another thirty minutes to his time. You wonder if he will be able to complete the day's schedule. **Go to 26**

21 You explain politely that the drums are needed in your daily work, and that it's not easy to give them away.

"I realise that, but you have quite a lot. One would really help me out."

Do you agree to give a drum?

Yes: go to 22   Maybe: 23   Otherwise go to 25

22

You decide that it's important to keep the air traffic controller happy. You invite him to come down to the truck and collect the empty drum. He takes it, lies it down, and starts rolling it towards the base of the control tower. You notice a few other drums stacked up there.

The aircraft leaves without incident, and you're soon back at your base. As you park the pickup truck your colleague walks past.

"Where's the second drum?" he asks. You explain what happened.

"Oh, you've got to be kidding me. Don't you see what you've done? They'll be all over us next time for more drums. And not just drums. Food donations, buckets, all sorts. Didn't you hear what I explained the other day?"

You try to explain that you wanted to keep the plane moving.

"You don't get it, do you? Once they know they can get something once, they'll always want something. I knew I should have gone myself." He pauses for a minute, and calms down.

"Look, I suppose it's not your fault. You're not used to dealing with these guys. But you've got to be strategic. You can't just go giving away things to everyone you meet. Now I'd better let the others know, so they can expect fresh demands the next time they go there."

He walks away towards the lunch room.

Go to 26

23

You think about the situation for a minute. You recall your colleague's warning about not creating a culture where people see things given away.

But you realise what a key role this controller has. As long as you continue to charter flights to reach your goal, your ability to operate smoothly will be affected by the controller. Various pilots have described to you the benefit of having air traffic control on their side.

You realise that if you brought the drum to his home, rather than giving it to him in public, that no-one else at the airport need know.

Do you offer to bring the drum to his home?

Yes: go to 24

Otherwise go to 25

24

You decide that it's important to keep the air traffic controller happy. You offer to drop the drum back to his home, explaining that you can't be seen to be giving away lots of agency equipment. He catches on immediately, and agrees.

You ask him to draw you a map of where his home is. While drawing the route, he calls his son to tell him that you'll be arriving soon.

When he ends the call he looks at you. "I'll spread the word that you're not to be bothered," he says. "If anyone asks you for something, tell them I said you shouldn't give things away. They'll understand."

The aircraft leaves without incident, and after a detour to drop off the drum at the air traffic controller's home, you're soon back at your base. As you park the pickup truck your colleague walks past.

"Where's the second drum?" he asks. You explain what happened. He looks at you for a moment.

"You know what, that was pretty smart. That controller's got a lot of power at the airport. If he tells everyone to leave us alone our job's going to be a lot easier. I can see why they said you were a good person to have on the team. I'll let the others know."

He walks away towards the lunch room.

Go to 26

25   As politely as you can you refuse his request.

For a moment he seems taken aback by your reply. Then he turns to the flight plan.

"Look, the pilot hasn't signed in the box. I can't file this."

You look at where he is pointing. A small part of the pilot's scribbled signature has gone outside of the signature box. You know that it's nothing. But, unfortunately, you know that the controller has the authority to release or hold planes on the tarmac.

"You'll need to get him to fill out a new one. Bring it back when you're done."

As you head down the steps you know the pilot is going to be really upset. The extra paperwork and the delay in submission will easily add another thirty minutes to his time. You wonder if he will be able to complete the day's schedule.

Go to 26

26 On the last day of their visit you invite the donors to join you on a medical delivery. You have a new staff member on the team and want to familiarise her with the distribution process.

Your normal refrigerated truck is still not ready, but the Landcruiser you used previously is available. From previous experience you know that using chiller boxes along with the vehicle's air conditioning is quite effective.

Part way into the journey Doug mentions that he changed his return flight and is now planning to leave in the evening. He asks if that is going to work. You realise that the timing is quite tight, but push the thought to the back of your mind. You're more concerned about keeping the medicines in good condition.

Three hours into the countryside, on a "safe" route, your truck is stopped by government soldiers at a checkpoint.

The soldiers are concerned about weapons being smuggled, and they want to open your vehicle and inspect every box.

You realise that if they do that, it will add at least almost an hour to your journey. In addition, by breaking the seal on the boxes, the medicine will spoil a lot quicker.

One of the soldiers mentions that if you just pay an "inspection fee" of $50, you can carry straight on.

Your passengers all have strong opinions on what to do. Doug wants to pay the soldiers from the supply of cash he carries for emergencies. He explains that this is an emergency, and the lives in the village are more important than the moral issue of paying a questionable fee.

One of your team members strongly disagrees. She explains that if you do this, you will set up the same thing to happen every time another agency comes by. And she explains that the soldiers might think that your agency is in fact smuggling weapons since you want to avoid the search.

You notice that your newest staff member, Carol, is very quiet. You're glad that it's one less opinion to deal with.

Do you allow Doug to pay the fine?

Yes: go to 27

Maybe: Go to 28

Otherwise go to 30

27

You tell Doug to pay the fine. The soldiers accept it and you drive on.

The medical delivery happens quickly, and the drive home passes without incident.

You pull into your compound and Doug heads towards the house to get his bags. The other passengers start unloading the empty chiller boxes.

Carol approaches you.

"That really bothered me to see what you did back there. In my last posting we never paid bribes. I don't think we should be taking this approach." She walks towards the office.

That evening, once Doug has left, you open your laptop to deal with your email. At the top of the items is an email from the regional manager. She wants to have a skype call tomorrow midday to discuss a complaint she's received from a staff member about cases of bribery.

You had been planning a hike to a nearby mountain with some friends as a means to release some stress. You realise that taking the skype call means you'll miss the trip. Your only consolation is that you know the regional manager is very experienced. You hope she'll be able to look at the incident with an open mind.

Go to 31

28

You discuss the issue further with the team. You explain that this is really a case of extortion – from the patients who will receive the medicine. The only way those patients can be sure of getting unspoiled medicine is if you pay the money.

Doug suggests paying now, and bringing a member of the Ministry of Health on the next trip

Do you pay the fine?

Yes: go to 29   **Otherwise go to 30**

29

You tell Doug to pay the fine. The soldiers accept it and you drive on.

The medical delivery goes well, and the drive home passes without incident.

You pull into your compound and Doug heads towards the house to get his bags. The other passengers start unloading the empty chiller boxes. As they do, Carol approaches you.

"At first I was really bothered by what you did back there. In my last posting we never paid bribes. I thought you were making a very poor decision. But on the drive home I realised that it's different here. I'm not saying I'm okay with paying money like that, but I'm glad we got the medicine to the clinic in a good state." She walks towards the office.

You lean on the Landcruiser's bonnet and wait for Doug to return. You wonder what you're going to say at the coordination meeting tomorrow, if the subject of checkpoints comes up. **Go to 31**

30

You find yourself in agreement with your colleague. "She's right," you tell the others. "If we do this we'll be setting up the same thing to happen every time another agency comes by. We have to think beyond the immediate. And I definitely don't want them thinking we've got something to hide. Let's help them open the boxes, and be as quick as we can."

Despite your involvement the search goes quite slowly. The afternoon is very hot and most of the soldiers are unwilling to leave the shade of their nearby building. The two who do get involved are more of a hindrance than a help, fiddling with the catches on the boxes, and double-checking boxes that have already been checked.

Eventually you leave, and drive on to the clinic. You unload the boxes and are relieved to see that most of the medicines appear to be okay.

You drive back as quickly as you can. Doug is agitated, tapping the dashboard and making faint clucking noises. His stress is infectious and you find yourself gripping the steering wheel very tensely. You're relieved to drop off your other colleagues as Doug rushes up to the house to collect his bags.

Driving speedily from the accommodation block, you weave through traffic and pull into the airport parking lot just in time to see Doug's plane lift off into the sky.

Doug turns to you.

"Great. Now I have to re-book my flight. The change fee is $100. I wish you had just let me pay those guys at the checkpoint. In my day we knew how to handle those situations."

You drive a very sullen Doug back to the compound for the night. He grabs his bags and strides off without a word. As you turn to lock the vehicle, Carol comes up to you.

"I just wanted to say, I thought you handled that situation today really well. I really respect how you stood firm in the face of bribery. It makes me feel good to be part of this team."

Go to 31

31

The last of the donors left in the early evening. You enjoyed their company, and learned from them, but you definitely found your other work backing up while you hosted them.

Although you're tired, you're looking forward to a brief visit with a colleague before you get some much-needed sleep. They recently returned from a break, and are known for bringing back good food and drink. You're sure that an hour in their company will be a good way to de-stress.

Just as you're about to leave there's a knock on your door. The compound guard is there, looking worried.

"We need you at the gate. They're saying they want to arrest Stephen and Carol."

"Who is? What's going on?"

"I'm not sure who they are. You'd better come."

Grabbing your phone and your handheld radio, you step out into the night and follow him down the path towards the main gate. The path isn't lit but the full moon overhead gives a good amount of light. As you walk, you wonder what could be happening. Stephen, an intern, has been with you for several months. You haven't had any problems with him. And Carol hasn't been around long enough to find herself in any trouble.

You reach the gate. Off to one side, deep in the shadows of the covered area you use for visitors to wait at, sit several men in military uniform. From what you can make out, the uniform is a pattern that you've seen a lot locally, but it's hard to tell in the weak light cast from the nearby guard hut. Opposite the men, looking very scared, are Carol and Stephen. The guard looks nervous too.

You approach the uniformed men, introduce yourself, and sit at the table. You ask what the problem is.

A skinny man in the middle of the group replies. He's clearly the one in charge.

"The problem is, these people are spies. They were taking photos at night. Who takes photos at night? I think they're working against the government."

You ask Stephen and Carol what he means. They explain that they had climbed the compound's water tower, several stories high, in order to take picture of the full moon and stars.

"I live behind that fence," the man continues, pointing in the direction of the water tower. "I work for the secret police. And I've never seen anyone take photos of the moon. Now I'm arresting these two, and they can tell their story to the court."

Stephen and Carol look extremely worried.

Do you offer to go in their place?

Yes: go to 32

Otherwise go to 33

32

You feel that you have a duty of care for your younger colleagues, and you feel you can handle the arrest better. You're especially concerned for the young intern, Stephen. He's not long out of college and he looks very frightened. You explain that you could go in their place.

The skinny man looks at you in surprise.

"No," he says, after a moment. "They're the criminals. They have to come."

Go to 33

33

At that moment the gate opens a fraction. As you watch, a colleague from another NGO, Akeem, walks in. You share the compound with the NGO, and several of their staff from different areas stay overnight before they head out to project sites.

You realise that Akeem is of the same ethnic background as the soldiers sitting in front of you. As he notices the soldiers he gives a small look of surprise, and starts to walk past. You wonder if he is frightened, or if he assumes you are doing some late business.

Do you ask him to join you?

Yes: go to 34

Otherwise go to 37

34

You ask Akeem to join you. He greets the soldiers and sits down next to you. You briefly explain what is happening, and then he and the soldiers start a lengthy discussion. You can't tell what is being said but you watch the body language closely.

After several minutes Akeem points at Stephen and laughs. The soldiers join in. You can't tell if it's cruel laughter, but the tension drops noticeably.

After a few more minutes' talking, the skinny soldier turns to you.

"It's okay. We won't take them. We'll go and tell our boss that it was a mistake."

Before you realise, they're on their feet and leaving. After they've gone, you turn to thank Akeem.

"Don't mention it," he says. He turns and walks towards the residence.

You spend a while talking with Carol and Stephen. They are clearly shaken, but you are able to help them understand that the threat has passed. You advise them each to make sure they talk to a friend about what happened, and tell them you'll discuss it more in the coming days.

The next afternoon you are busy with a financial report. Your colleague informs you that the skinny soldier is back.

You step out to the seating area, and find three soldiers sitting there. In the bright daylight their uniforms look dishevelled, and their eyes have drawn, tired looks.

They greet you in a friendly way, and tell you a little about their other activities during the night. One of them makes a point of showing you his handgun, and explains that they're always armed. You realise they might be one reason why the streets around your location have been calm at night, even though you've been hearing security reports of violent break-ins in other suburbs.

After a bit more talking, the leader reveals what is clearly the purpose of their follow-up visit.

"As we told Akeem, we're prepared to leave your colleagues alone. Everyone who's young is stupid. We can't expect them to act like adults. But my commander still needs them to pay the fine. It's a hundred dollars. I can take it to him."

You're surprised , since you thought the issue was resolved. You start to weigh things up – the usefulness of having a local group like this on your side, the subtle hint of the threat that came with showing the handgun, the repercussions if you don't pay.

Do you make the payment?

Yes: go to 35

Otherwise go to 36

35

You realise there is no way the situation is going away. You decide to accept it as a cost of having interns and new staff. Particularly in the intern's case, he's produced far more than $100 worth of work.

You hand over the money, explaining that you'll tell your staff to be a lot more careful in the future. You also ask for assurances that you'll be informed if there's another problem, before it gets to this stage. The skinny soldier agrees.

Over the next few months the soldiers visit from time to time. Although you don't particularly enjoy their visits, they share a lot of helpful information with you – about which suburbs are becoming riskier, which types of crime are on the increase, and other similar issues. You realise that in the absence of a strong police force, it is probably quite helpful to have them on side with you.

Ends.

36
You have no way of knowing where the money will go. Clearly, it's not the sort of payment that has a receipt with it. You remember that Akeem had come in to your finance office to pay one of his agency's bills. He might still be there. You ask the soldiers to excuse you for a minute, and walk up the steps to the finance office.

To your relief Akeem is still there, going through some receipts. You explain the latest development to him, and ask him if he can help.

"You don't understand, do you? This isn't optional. This is how things work here. You need to pay them the fine. This won't go away until you do."

You look at him for a moment. You really trust his judgement. He's been a great guide to the culture to you on several previous occasions.

You resign yourself to paying, and ask your finance office for the money.

Go to 35

37
Suddenly the skinny soldier becomes very aggressive.

"You're wasting our time. You can pay a fine right now, two hundred dollars. Or we take them both to prison."

Do you pay the fine?

Yes? Go to 38   Otherwise go to 39

38 You realise there is no way the situation is going away. You decide to accept it as a cost of having interns and new staff. Particularly in the intern's case, he's produced far more than $200 worth of work.

You hand over the money, explaining that you'll tell your staff to be a lot more careful in the future. The soldiers calm down considerably.

You also ask for assurances that you'll be informed if there's another problem, before it gets to this stage. The skinny soldier agrees.

Over the next few months the soldiers visit from time to time. Although you don't particularly enjoy their visits, they share a lot of helpful information with you – about which suburbs are becoming riskier, which types of crime are on the increase, and other similar issues. You realise that in the absence of a strong police force, it is probably quite helpful to have them on side with you.

Ends.

39

You feel that the soldiers are trying to bully you all. "I can't pay this. It's not a proper process. These staff haven't done anything wrong, they're not spies."

The soldiers stand up. One of them pulls a pair of handcuffs from a pouch at his side.

"If that's how you feel, we're taking them."

You hear a sobbing beside you. Stephen, the young intern, has tears running down his face.

"We were just taking photos. It was just a nice moon, that's all. I don't want to go to prison." He pulls out his wallet. "I have two hundred here. Just take it, okay. I'm sorry. It won't happen again."

The skinny soldier reaches across and takes the money from him. Glaring at you all, he tells his men they are leaving.

"We'll be keeping an eye on you all. If I see any more spying there'll be real problems." He walks towards the gate.

You spend the next few hours sitting with Stephen and Carol, helping them calm down. Stephen's really shaken, and you wonder how badly the incident is going to affect the rest of his time working with you. The first hint of dawn is brushing the sky by the time you finally get to your accommodation. Exhausted, you go straight to bed.

Ends.

Gifts and bribes

What is a gift? What is a bribe? What is a reasonable payment to allow a vital service to continue?

Almost all cultures give gifts. Birthday presents and wedding presents are two common examples. Sometimes gifts are freely given, with no expectation of anything in return. But not all giving is devoid of selfish motivation: parents may give extravagant gifts in the hope of winning their children's love; relatives may give lavish gifts at a public gathering such as a wedding as a way of displaying their wealth and success.

Many cultures cement business relationships through gift-giving. Companies hold tickets to 'director's boxes' or courtside seats where they can entertain favoured clients. Airlines reward frequent customers with more exclusive facilities.

In many cultures people working in certain roles expect small gifts, even if it is not written in law. Paying a small tip, for example, is commonplace in a multitude of settings. Waiting staff, hotel staff, and others are all inclined to treat tipping customers more favourably than those who withhold tips.

Even within a small team from the same culture, it is common to find a number of differing answers to the question of whether a payment is a gift or a bribe. Considering that relief work is often made up of teams from multiple countries and cultures, each used to different norms of behaviour, and all working in yet another culture, it is clear that defining the "right" viewpoint towards payment is impossible.

It can greatly help your decision making at the point of a demand for payment if you have developed a basic understanding of different payment types, and how different cultures view them. Combining this with an understanding of your approach, your colleagues' approach, your agency's approach, and the specific culturally appropriate approach can help you rapidly respond in the face of a demand.

Making a distinction

There are different ways to judge whether a payment is a gift or a bribe. One way which some people find helpful is to consider the following distinction:

Are you paying for services to which you're entitled, or are you paying for unlawful treatment?

If you go to take your driving licence, and pass the test, you're entitled to a licence under the laws of the country. Having paid the published fee in order to take the test, you have a legal right to the licence. However, if the clerk asks for a personal tip or they won't print the licence, they are holding back a service to which you are entitled.

A different situation is where you go in to take the test, but, doubting your ability to successfully pass the test, you initiate an offer to pay the clerk privately for the licence in order to avoid taking the test.

In the first case, you are forced to make a supplementary payment for a service to which you are already legally entitled.

In the second case, you are offering payment for an advantage to which you are not legally entitled.

You could consider the first situation to be a case of extortion, which forces you to pay. Sometimes extortion is blatant and involves the threat of physical harm, such as a policeman who threatens arrest on made-up charges unless a payment is made. Other times it threatens inconvenience, or added expense, such as the customs official who threatens an expensive and time-consuming trip to the capital city to sort out paperwork if a payment isn't made.

The second situation involves a bribe. You are not legally entitled to the driving licence unless you take the driving test. By making a payment you are bypassing a legal requirement.

In considering whether to make a payment, it can be helpful to discover what type of situation you are facing. Is it a case of extortion, where you have little choice but to pay? Or is it one where you are paying for an unfair advantage?

Finally there is a middle ground, which involves 'facilitation fees.' These are recognised payments which allow you to speed up a process. Open examples include airlines which allow payment of a 'priority boarding' fee in order to allow you to bypass long check-in lines. Less open examples exist where payment is widely made and generally acknowledged, but may not be documented.

Corruption Response Scale

What about general gift-giving? How appropriate is it? Is your gift-giving genuine, in your culture, in your colleagues' cultures, and in the host culture? Or is it paying for an unfair advantage? What if it is one thing to you and another thing to your colleague? What is your agency's position?

To avoid being paralysed at the decision-making stage it can be helpful to consider a simple model, developed specifically to understand the process.

At one extreme we have a person from a very black and white culture. Their approach is, if there isn't a receipt for the payment, it's not acceptable. In their view the idea of giving a gift, even one to cement a relationship, is bribery.

Their approach can be represented as a line on which actions are either permissible (white) or non-permissible (black). There is no area of circumstantial ambiguity.

If you had to draw their position on the chart, it would look like this:

At the other extreme is someone who would make a payment under any circumstances, if it was required to achieve the task. They might make some payments (white), more readily than others (light grey), but there are no non-permissible (black) points for them.

Their position on the chart would look like this:

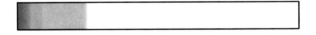

In between the two positions is someone from a culture where gift-giving is an acceptable practice in certain situations, particularly where there is an ongoing relationship. They might make a tip at Christmas time to the rubbish collectors, the mail delivery person, and so on. They would not expect a receipt in these situations. However, there are plenty of situations where they would not consider it appropriate to make a payment.

Their position on the chart would be represented as:

Finally, consider someone from a culture where gift-giving extends quite broadly. They would make a payment in a number of situations that people from some cultures would find questionable. But there are certain situations where they would draw the line.

Their position on the chart looks more like:

Putting the different standpoints together gives an overall scale:

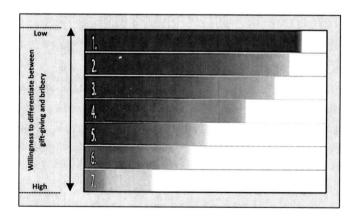

Figure 5.1 The foundation of the Corruption Response Scale

Using the scale, a person's approach to corruption can be described as a value from 1 to 7, representing the degree of willingness with which that approach distinguishes between gift-giving and bribery.

In order for the scale to be complete, there is one further aspect of corruption to mention. All references to this point have been to gift giving which is to some extent voluntary. An individual can refuse to make a payment, although doing so may result in a great deal of inconvenience. However, situations also occur where an individual is forced, under duress, to make a payment. These situations are referred to as extortion, and the individual has very little choice about making the required payment.

Even in situations of extortion, individual responses may vary, with those who take a stricter view being willing to suffer to a greater extent before they 'compromise their principles.' A similar chart can be made of approaches to extortion, although fewer possible responses exist.

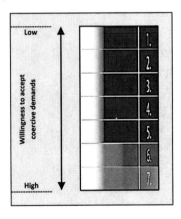

Figure 5.2 The extortion component of the Corruption Response Scale

Extortion will either be given in to or not, although those adopting the situational approach may give in to extortion more readily than others. In the preceding chart (figure 5.2), black indicates a refusal to give in to extortion, and white is the point at which the individual has no option but to give in. The shades of grey highlight the blurred distinction some approaches make regarding the point at which an individual is forced to give in.

The two parts of the scale can then be joined together to describe the range of possible distinctions between gift-giving and bribery (figure 5.3).

The Corruption Response Scale allows you, by asking yourself a few simple questions (appendix A), to arrive at an approximate position on the scale.

This forms the starting point in understanding how to make decisions where different viewpoints about gift-giving and bribery exist. You might come to identify yourself as being a [2] on the scale, or a [5], or even a [7], depending on your particular background.

You can then go on to ask yourself what position your colleagues are likely to occupy on the scale, informally evaluating their behaviour using the same questions. This will give you a rough idea, before a situation is encountered, of the likelihood of a conflict occurring between your choice of action and that of your colleague(s). By anticipating a conflict ahead of its occurrence, you become forewarned and better able to resolve it.

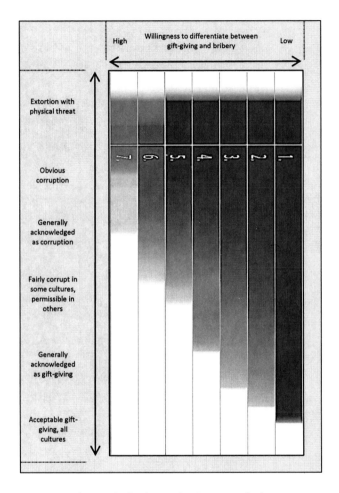

Figure 5.3 The Corruption Response Scale

Organisations and other cultures

The Corruption Response Scale can also be applied to your organisation. This can help you see if your approach fits with theirs, and predict any potential clashes. However, unlike individuals, agencies tend to occupy a range of positions on the scale, for they usually accommodate individuals with a wide variety of approaches.

As an example, an international organisation headed by humanitarian workers with significant experience may prefer to operate as a [3]. In recognition of the challenges in their work, they may allow managers the freedom to operate as a [4] or a [5]. They may also accommodate members who take a stricter view and so they encompass [2] within their range. Nonetheless, they would find [1] to be unrealistically strict given their cross-cultural locations, and they would consider [7] to be too liberal. Rather than a number, such an organisation can be said to occupy a *range* of values. Imposed on the scale, the organisation would appear as below, occupying the non-blurred lines [2 - 5] (figure 5.4)

Finally, you can use the scale to broadly evaluate the culture you are working in. This will help you identify in advance if there is a fundamental clash between your agency's position and the predominant position held by most people in the host culture.

With all this in mind you can predict how you will respond to a sudden demand for payment. You can look at the team you are with, and judge how supportive your colleagues are likely to be of your decision. You can predict areas where you may face conflict with your organisation if you make a particular choice. You can even look at areas where choices by your own organisation will lead it into conflict with a different agency, which takes either a stricter or a much more relaxed approach to bribery.

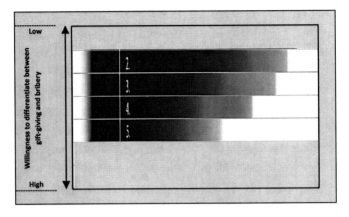

Figure 5.4 An agency permits a range of approaches on the Corruption Response Scale

All of this increased understanding will accelerate your move towards expertise, since a component of expertise is recognising and perceiving situations. As you apply this increased clarity of understanding, you will find that the process of making decisions that relate to issues of bribery and gift-giving becomes much easier.

Changing positions on the scale

It is important to consider that a person or organisation's position on the Corruption Response Scale can change. Some of these changes may be temporary and some may be permanent. To help your level of understanding and improve your decision making, note that the change may occur in you, your colleagues, or your organisation, depending on the situation.

Temporary shifts can occur in relation to a particular situation. For example, a person may usually limit their practice of giving relationship-cementing gifts to situations where their aim is to develop a genuine long-term relationship. However, in reaction to the pressures found in disaster relief, that same person may be forced to give similar gifts without any anticipation of a relationship developing. They will only be in a location temporarily, and their desire to save lives may cause them to make a payment to ensure that the process moves along swiftly. The short-term goal of expediting a process has taken priority over their intention to build a relationship.

The person in question has moved to a lower position on the vertical scale (for example, from a [2] to a [5]), driven by the external pressures of working in disaster relief. The change is temporary because the individual, when returning to a more stable environment, will revert to the vertical position which they adopted before their involvement with the relief situation. Developing your expertise in this comes by observing how some colleagues may change their approach based on the urgency and size of human consequences present in a situation.

In similar fashion, an organisation as a whole can change its position on the scale. For example, an international development organisation may choose to move into short-term relief projects in conflict environments. In response to the greater pressures found in disaster response, the organisation's headquarters may give field staff more discretionary power to deal with corrupt situations on a case-by-case basis. In this case, the organisation has expanded from [2 - 3] to [2 - 5].

A permanent change can occur when a person experiences influences such as prolonged exposure to a worldview different to their own, or a sudden event which dramatically changes how they view the world. Generally, experienced cross-cultural humanitarian workers show a trend of moving to a higher number on the scale over time, highlighting a shift away from a more black and white viewpoint. Anticipating this in an experienced colleague can help you predict how they may behave at a decision point.

For organisations, permanent shifts may occur in response to guidelines or 'codes of conduct' which have the effect of modifying an industry's behaviour over time. They may also occur in response to official legislation, such as the Bribery Act 2010, which affects British charities working abroad. The impact of the UK's Bribery Act is to effectively remove some of the higher numbers on the scale as being acceptable approaches, so an organisation may be forced to narrow its range from [2 - 6] to [2 - 4].

General advice

It is not the place of this chapter to suggest a particular approach to gift-giving. Rather, the aim is to improve your decision-making ability by helping you understand some of the conflict points which may arise, and why.

Nonetheless, there are a few general points that may be helpful to bear in mind as you develop your own position with regards to gift-giving:

1. Think of the particular culture you are in. Is it culturally appropriate to give small gifts? When does this occur? In business? Socially?

2. Think about your relative wealth. Both as an individual and as an organisation. Many times you will be wealthier than many of the people in the culture that you have come to. What do wealthy people do in the culture? For example, do wealthy people give tips? For what types of activities?

3. Think about the precedent you set when you give a gift. Are you tying up all your future activities, and those of other organisations, to the payment of gifts?

4. Think about the size of the gift. Is this something appropriate or is it going to create greed? For example, the checkpoint guard who has stopped you: have they been standing there in the sun all day, with nothing but warm water? Do you have a cold can of soda that would make a big difference to them? Is that something that you could buy cheaply beforehand that would ease a negotiation? Thinking creatively for ways to give genuine signs of friendship, as opposed to money, can go a long way.

5. Think about the person's overall situation: Is it a policeman who hasn't been paid for months – but whose extended family is relying on them to provide food and pay school fees? Is the individual themselves corrupt, or are they a product of a corrupt situation which has left them using their authority for their own survival? What do they think when they see you rush in to help

destitute people – when their own family is almost as destitute? Is there a way to support them at their level, without compromising your own or your organisation's approach?

6. Finally, a very simple test is whether or not the gift can be given openly. Generally speaking, the more openly the exchange can be made, the more likely it is to be a gift.

Gift-giving is a challenging subject, and those working on the frontline of humanitarian response can expect to be faced with the issue repeatedly. Developing an understanding of the different responses available – your own, those of your colleagues, and that of your organisation – is an important step towards effective decision making. As you return to the scenario for a second time, try to evaluate how your own position on the Corruption Response Scale is affecting your decisions.

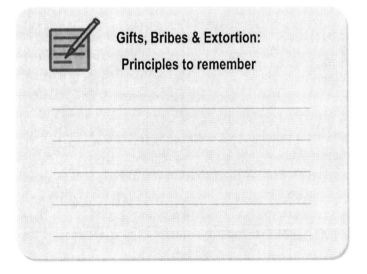

Gifts, Bribes & Extortion:
Principles to remember

CHAPTER FIVE

ORGANISATIONAL
POLICIES

Disaster **response** is by its nature a challenging environment in which to work. Having a strong, committed team with high internal trust can make things a lot easier. Yet many issues are forced on team members and team leaders by an organisation's policies. While these policies may be well-meaning, they often fail to take into account the complexities of field work. Holding strictly to all policies may actually erode the trust which a good team needs.

Understanding the basis for your organisation's policies can help you respond to the tension that they often create. It can also help you identify solutions that in turn become an obvious choice when a decision needs to be made.

Scenario Five

You've been dealing with the refugee crisis (Scenario Two) for several weeks now. Your supply lines have improved, and many of the tents at the train yard have been replaced by molded plastic sheds. These sheds do a much better job of keeping occupants dry, and hold a reasonable amount of warmth. This has become important since increasing numbers of families are choosing to spend the night in the sheds, giving them a full day to walk the mountain track after a night's rest. You are glad to see this change, since the nights have become extremely cold, and the track is often covered in ice and snow. Due to the conditions the government have cancelled the night trains, and the last arrivals now come by 7pm. You have found that three hours is plenty of time to get the new arrivals fed, given new clothes, and those who need accommodation settled.

With your agency being so thinly stretched responding to other crises, you're still heavily reliant on volunteers, but you have been able to recruit a few more permanent staff members. Unfortunately many of them lack experience in disaster response, and are using the current crisis as a means to secure a first job.

You've been able to secure a large motel in the nearby town further down the mountain, which serves as your accommodation, office, and general storehouse. Although the owners are welcoming, you've noticed a shift in recent weeks in the attitude of the townspeople. Many are unemployed, and there is a clear resentment about the amount that is being done for those passing through further up the mountain. The situation hasn't been helped by the partying attitude adopted by some groups of volunteers. You know of one volunteer organisation that just expelled two of its volunteers after they were caught at the end of a night drinking trying to carry off the statue of a local war hero. At the weekly security meeting one well-respected NGO reported that one of their staff members was robbed while walking back from the convenience store.

You discussed these developments with your regional manager, and they have instructed you to put a 10pm curfew in place for all activities, both work and social. The drive from the camp down the mountain only takes fifteen minutes, so you can finish your work two and a half hours after the last train and still easily be back before curfew.

You finish a long, tiring shift at the transit camp and climb into the back of the minibus. It sets off down the mountain, and before you know it you are back at the motel. The minibus pulls into the motel parking area. As you climb out and pull on your warm jacket, a staff member approaches you. They've only been on the team for about a week. You know they weren't on the shift that just finished with you.

"I know it's getting late, but I wanted to go and get a pizza at that bar down the road. They've got a real pizza oven. And the tap beer's not bad either. I don't think I can stomach another night of two-minute noodles."

You know the bar they mean; you've been there yourself for pizza from time to time. It's quite a rough place. You look at your watch: 9.55pm. Yesterday evening you enforced the curfew and two of your staff were very unhappy about it.

Do you allow the staff member to go?

Yes: go to 1　　　**Maybe: go to 2**　　　**Otherwise go to 5**

1 You decide to let them go. You didn't set the curfew, you didn't appreciate all the complaining from the group you said no to last night, and you don't want to face the same thing again.

As the new staff member walks towards the motel exit, you're joined by two others.

"So why is he allowed to go out? We weren't – and he's brand new. Why the double standards?"

You struggle to justify your approach to the complaining staff. You realise it's going to be hard to enforce the curfew in the coming days.

Go to 5

2 You ask them what is most important – the pizza or the beer.

"Well, the beer would be nice, sure. But mostly I'm just sick of noodles. I would have gone earlier but one of the other teams needed help loading blankets for tomorrow's shift. We haven't stopped for the last two hours."

One of the senior staff is unloading the minibus. They've been on location for several weeks, have picked up a few of the local greetings, and generally seem very reliable.

Do you ask the senior staff member to go on a pizza run to collect some takeaways?

Yes: go to 3   **No: go to 4**

3 You explain the situation to the experienced staff member.

"Sure, no problem. I'll do a quick check and see if anyone else wants takeaways too." They head off across the parking lot. As they walk towards the motel exit, you're joined by two other staff members.

"So why are they allowed to go out? We weren't. Why the double standards?"

Quickly and directly, you point out the staff member's experience, reliability, and the fact that they had no interest in staying out for a drink. You tell the two staff that when they've been in place for as long, that you'll consider their options too. You lock up the minibus and head towards your room.
Go to 5

4 "Sorry," you tell the new staff member, "but the curfew is the curfew. If I let you break it then tomorrow night everyone's going to want to break it. I don't make the rules here, but I am responsible for seeing that they're followed."

You lock up the minibus and prepare to go back to your room. But then you decide to wait a while by the motel's entrance to make sure the curfew is followed. You don't want staff members undermining your authority. As you stand in the gloom, legs tired and feet sore from a day on your feet, you find yourself wondering if you signed up to emergency relief in order to work as a curfew-enforcer. You feel more like a school playground supervisor than a humanitarian worker.
Go to 5

5   Two days later you are up at the mountain transit camp, inside the camp manager's portacabin. You have joined a number of other agencies for a weekly coordination meeting. Different groups mention the work they are doing, and the goods that they either have or are planning to bring.

The leader of a well-respected international NGO, Life for Children, mentions that the night trains have started running again. She mentions being quite overwhelmed since most groups have now moved away from night shifts. Looking at you, she asks if your agency can start operating again. She points out that your staff were always really welcoming to the people they served, and seemed willing to do as much as required to solve people's problems.

You explain that you'd like to help, but that your agency has quite a strict policy. Because you are now in a curfew situation, operations are not allowed during curfew hours until there is a site inspection from the regional security manager. You point out that the security manager is due in the following week. They are currently travelling to the different sites, and out of contact.

The manager at Life for Children says she understands, but asks you to check with your regional manager if there is any way you can work outside the curfew. The needs are much more pressing at night, she says. You assure her that you will check.

That afternoon, at your team meeting, you brief your staff on the latest developments. Several of them mention how good it was working at night, and point out that they never felt at any real risk. The trouble, one person says, is down in the town, not at the site itself. You have been trying your manager by phone and by email, but you have been unable to get through or receive a reply.

Do you decide to start helping again at night, without the security manager's approval?

Yes: go to 6   Maybe: go to 7   Otherwise go to 9

6 You consider the general willingness from the staff in the room, and the high reported need up on the mountain. You also remember how safe you generally felt while working in at the transit site.

You decide that you will start night shifts again, due to the pressing need. The first two nights go very well. Your team are energised to be working in the high-pressure situation. When you look around and only see your team alongside the team from Life for Children, you realise how vital it is that you are there.

After the second night of work you return to your room at the motel. Glancing at your email before you go to sleep, you notice an email from your regional headquarters.

It seems that the regional security manager has heard that you are operating outside the curfew. Your manager at headquarters writes that this is an unacceptable breach of security policy. In response they are planning to bring in a "more experienced" manager to take over your role, as soon as they finish their annual leave. They will allow you to stay on, but in a deputy role to the new manager once they arrive.

Go to 10

7

You consider asking all staff who want to work to sign a disclaimer, saying that they are working of their own choice and releasing the agency from any responsibility. You recall that a recent case of a staff member suing an agency for negligence has caused a greater climate of risk-aversion in many agencies.

When you mention the suggestion to your team they respond very positively, all agreeing that they are willing to sign a waiver in order to get on with the work.

Do you ask staff to sign a waiver and then recommence the night shifts?

Yes: go to 6

Maybe: go to 8

Otherwise go to 9

8 You try to think of the situation from your agency's perspective. You realise that having a security assessment is important to them. You inform your team that you'll have an update before the evening shift, and tell those who want to work to be prepared for work at night

You make a quick call to the manager of Life for Children, asking if they have done a security assessment. She tells you that they have, and that they would be happy to share it with you. She emails it to you within minutes. You send the assessment to your regional manager and the security manager.

Shortly before the night shift is due to start you get a call from the regional manager. They are grateful to receive Life for Children's assessment, and agree that it will cover the purpose. They wish you luck as you resume your night work. **Go to 10**

9 You decide that your agency must have a reason for requiring a security assessment. You're not willing to re-start operations until after the security manager's visit the following week. You inform your team that you won't be working at night until after that.

That evening two of your more trusted volunteers come to see you. They inform you that they're leaving the organisation because they feel it is too risk averse. They explain that another NGO has said they can join as volunteers, and join the night shift to help cover the urgent needs. They apologise for leaving at short notice but explain that they came to work, not to be bound up by bureaucracy. **Go to 10**

10

A few nights later you're back at the camp. The local government notice requesting all agencies to resume night work has cleared the way for your team to be there. Your agency has responded positively to the request, even though they have a few questions about overall safety. The government have put on extra trains, and the numbers of people flooding through the transit stop are much higher than they were before.

To gain some measure of control, the government have installed a series of crowd control barriers at the start of the mountain track. There's a heavy police presence, and at times the police have started checking people's documents. This has created a bottleneck of refugees in the train sidings. Penned in by the mountain wall on one side, and the aid agency tents on the other, people are spilling back towards the platform.

The camp is busy with volunteers, but people are having a hard time keeping up with the crowd surges. Before one train load has been fully processed and given food and clothing, another set of carriages arrive. A worried-looking volunteer pushes through the crowd to the food tent where you are busy serving.

"We need more people on crowd control. We've got to split people into groups or someone's going to get crushed. We need experienced people like you. Can you get someone to cover for you? We need your help."

You follow him out of the food tent and push your way through the crowd. He motions to where a tall, pale volunteer in a fluorescent yellow vest is standing with arms outstretched.

"Can you help Tom? He's can't control this stage by himself."
He pushes his way further into the crowd and disappears.

You spend most of the night holding back surges of people.
Most groups respond to your requests and do their best to
hold back, but sometimes you have to physically push back
against the pressing crowd. You worry about what would
happen if you lost your balance or got caught up against the
rock wall during a crowd surge.

At some point in the night the generator goes out, and for
about half an hour there is almost total darkness. You're
grateful for your head-torch and are glad that you insisted all
staff carry a flashlight.

At your team debrief the next morning, one of the volunteers
mentions that she felt very vulnerable during the power cut.
When she left the clothing tent to get more deliveries she
was grabbed several times as she moved through the crowd.

Another staff member says they heard that even more
refugees are expected that night.

The team ask if they are going to be working that night, in
light of the security risks.

Will you continue to work as things are?

Yes: go to 11

Maybe: go to 12

Otherwise go to 14

11
You decide the needs at night are too important to ignore. You consider that the risks are worth taking.

Two nights later, in the middle of a snowstorm, the freezing crowd stampedes. It's hard to tell where exactly it starts, but soon the whole corridor to the mountain track is one big crush. The police gates are forced open and people pour down the track.

One the chaos has passed, you find your colleague on the ground, grunting from the pain of a broken leg. He had fallen in the surge, and his leg has been trampled.

You arrange emergency transport down the mountain to the local clinic. Thankfully a skeleton staff is working through the night and they are soon able to treat your injured colleague.

In the morning you phone the regional manager to give an update. Shortly afterwards you receive an email from the regional security officer. They inform you that all night operations must now be completed halted, regardless of any government requests.

You wonder how your team are going to take the news. Some may be relieved, but you are sure that some others are going to start looking for another agency to work with.

Ends.

12

As you think through the risks if you continue to work, an experienced staff member speaks up.

"When we worked in the refugee crisis last year, we had what we called a traffic light system. If conditions were green we worked as normal. If they were orange we had to work in pairs, and there were certain areas where only men could work. If conditions were red that meant all staff had to pull back to a safe location. It worked really well. We all knew what was going on, the camp manager used to walk around and mention how things were and let us know if there were any changes. Do you think we could put something like that in place. For the whole camp if they want it. Or at least for our team?"

Do you try implementing a traffic light system as she suggests?

Yes: go to 13

Otherwise go to 14

13

You decide to start using the system. You gather your team around and work out a simple series of actions for an 'orange' and a 'red' situation.

Once you have the ideas jotted down, you ask the lady who mentioned the idea to write a summary email to your regional HQ, describing what you have put in place.

Two nights later, in the middle of a snowstorm, you sense a growing tension in the air. Parents complain about needing blankets for their children, and groups of young men try to force their way to the front of the queue. To make it worse the fuel runs out, the generator stops working and the transit area is plunged into darkness. You quickly radio your team that the situation has moved to orange. Soon after, the freezing crowd stampedes. It's hard to tell where exactly it starts, but soon the whole corridor to the mountain track is one big crush. The police gates are forced open and people pour down the track.

In the aftermath, once the whole crowd has dispersed, you move through the transit area, checking on your team. To your relief they are all fine. Several thank you for the radio warning. You can see them growing in confidence as they successfully come through a difficult situation.

Ends.

14

You decide that it is too risky to continue night operations. Your team moves to daytime operations only.

In the nearby café where you often take meals, you hear a lot of NGO workers talking about the experiences at the transit site during the night. It sounds like that is where the bulk of the work is. You sense a growing disappointment amongst your team.

Three days later a group of volunteers asks to sit down with you. They had all come together by van from a neighbouring country, and have been a great help in the work. They inform you that they're leaving in order to join one of the big agencies that runs the child reception centre during the night.

You wonder how much of your team is going be left if this keeps up. You start writing an email to the regional office, requesting more staff.

Ends.

Organisational policies

Part of making good decisions at the frontline involves understanding your organisation's policies. In addition to reading the organisation's handbook, try to talk with experienced team members to find out how strict these policies are. By spending a bit of time reflecting on your situation, it should be possible to work out which policies are helping your team, and which ones may need to be adapted.

A recurring feature in disaster response situations is the presence of a high level of change. Situations change rapidly, and many times this means that the organisation's goals change too. Security may increase or decrease rapidly, and a host government may impose sudden legislative changes. In such situations, it may be more effective to have clear guidelines and principles, rather than a set of rigid rules. Where a policy either appears too restrictive, or is clearly hindering your team's operation, it may be sensible to approach your headquarters with suggestions for the policy's alteration. It can be helpful to support your proposal with examples of what other organisations in the same location are doing.

If your headquarters is unable or unwilling to relax certain rules, you may find yourself in situations where you are having to handle competing influences. Your organisation may be committed to helping the neediest people in a situation, yet its safety management policies may prevent you undertaking those life-saving activities. In the same way that values sometimes have to be set against each other, and objectives sometimes have to be compromised on, so policies also have to be balanced.

One way to avoid being paralysed at the decision-making

point is to develop an understanding of which policies take precedence over others. Some vocal members within the organisation may make the case for their policies more loudly, but try to maintain a focus on the overall objective. Talking with long-term team members can be a helpful way of working out the balance.

Creating policies

In some situations, particularly where there are concerns about the personal security of team members, you may find yourself involved in creating policies. Time spent in reflection at this point can make subsequent decisions much easier to make. Generally speaking, it is far easier to support a decision that you believe strongly in, compared to one where you feel a different outcome is better.

One method to make subsequent decisions in fast-changing situations easier is to avoid creating firm rules where possible. Instead provide positive principles:

- "For the sake of others we don't encourage selfish behavior."
- "Our exemptions are based on maturity or length of service."

In the second example above, having some exemptions can be particularly useful in situations where staff generally develop a good sense of security over time. Typically this would involve less secure locations. In such cases the type of exemption could be: In your first year of contract, you follow the organisation's rules; from the second year onwards, there are some simple guidelines; and the 'probation' period is reduced from one year to three months for experienced staff joining from other agencies.

Applying policies

Remember that your agency has a duty of care to all its staff; it also has its reputation to consider. When forced to make a decision which may differ from your agency's directive, try to find solutions which take these issues into account.

If you are forced to make decisions about a policy that you don't really support, it can be easier to have a planned response, to give you some time to consider changes. Examples could include:

1. If issues come up regularly, discuss the agency guidelines with senior team members at a special meeting.

2. Ask for suggestions from the local team, and guidance from HQ, on what flexibility could be built in to the policies.

3. Consider reasonable cut-off points in policies: how long does someone have to serve before they are considered for special exemption?

4. Have some standard responses ready:

   - "I can't agree to that right now, and I don't have time to discuss it, but give me 48 hours and I'll make sure we get a chance to discuss it. Try to bring me some suggestions on how the policy could be adapted."

- "That might seem odd to you as a new arrival. But spend the first four weeks just learning. A lot of the reasons will become clear to you. If it still seems unreasonable, come back to me and we'll discuss your thoughts."

Developing some personal strategies for these decision points will help you to maintain trust within the team while looking for solutions.

Different contexts

One important point to hold in mind is that policy-makers often develop policies in more predictable settings. For example, the organisation's policies on logistics and procurement may assume a fairly stable environment. As a result they will rely on certain assumptions, such as expecting that a country's stated import procedures will be adhered to, or that all merchants have recognisable invoicing procedures and documents in place.

The reality of a post-disaster situation is that many of these systems may have broken down. In the process of importing a vehicle or a large supply of goods, you may discover that the procedure is a lot more convoluted than expected. The sudden volume of imports may have caused a backlog, or the systems that allow importation to happen may themselves be damaged. In the process of making a large purchase, you may find that the local banking system is affected, and merchants will demand funding in cash, at levels that your organisation would normally expect to pay by cheque. There may be no recognisable receipting for some goods, other than photos of the goods themselves or a scrawled note on an unofficial document.

In these unstable situations, you can often find yourself caught between trying to adhere to your organisation's policies, and the reality of life on the ground. However, there are three basic steps that you can take in such situations that will help you in your overall decision making.

Firstly, as soon as you recognise the reality of an unstable situation, try to inform your organisation at a senior level. Explain the reality that you are facing and document it with a request that senior management provide you with a certain amount of leeway to deal with the situation. Doing this from a position of experience can be easier, but even as a newly arrived staff member you can encourage colleagues into a more understanding position if you document the particular limitations that you are encountering.

Secondly, understand that many times a situation will unfold, rather than be clear from the outset. For example, the procedures around the importing of your emergency response vehicle may be clear in general, but the specifics will be a lot more convoluted. Expect to allow longer than you had first estimated. Furthermore, try to become comfortable with processes that unfold one step at a time. Keep in mind the end goal of the process while maintaining a degree of flexibility about the process itself.

Finally, accept that you do not need to understand one hundred percent of what is taking place in a situation. If you have a colleague who is trusted in their role, and they are going through a very complicated process in order to achieve a task, keep your focus on the outcome. This is even more important where language barriers are involved. It can be tempting to try to understand exactly why a certain step in a process is delayed. But if your understanding of the matter will have no effect on its speed of eventual resolution, it can often be better to focus your mental energy on other tasks. By its very nature disaster response involves uncertainty. In that environment of overall uncertainty, you should take comfort in the fact that it's not realistic to expect to know everything about every process.

Disaster response is chaotic, and inevitably this can lead to tension between organisational policies and front line activities. To work effectively in this tension, aim to use your organisation's policies as good benchmarks to guide you in your work. Create a better decision-making environment by informing senior colleagues about any anticipated uncertainty or likely deviation from policy. Seek advice from experienced colleagues within your organisation and elsewhere. Above all, aim to keep the overall goal in mind and do all you can within the limits of safety to reach that goal.

Organisational Policies:
Principles to remember

CHAPTER SIX

PERCEPTIONS

Disaster response **almost always** involves an element of
cross-cultural work. Apart from those who respond
entirely in their own country – such as members of a civil
defence team – all frontline humanitarian responders are
going to encounter cultures different to their own.

The challenges you face in disaster response are
amplified by the perceptions that others have of you. How
you manage these perceptions – reinforcing any positive
perceptions of your role, and actively working to redress those
which are unfounded – will have a significant impact on your
effectiveness. Anticipating how an action will be perceived
should always be a part of your decision-making process.

Scenario Six

You're enjoying a well-earned day off from the various food and medical distributions (Scenario Four). Just going to your friend's house gives you a sense of escape from the work, and they have a good collection of DVDs and a bookshelf full of novels. Stretching out in the children's paddling pool in the back yard isn't the same as swimming, but the yard is private and secluded, and the pool's water offers a welcome break from the heat.

As you step inside to grab a drink, your phone rings. The screen shows it's Michel. You groan. It's bound to be his motorbike again. It's broken down several times and he always calls to see if you can come with the pickup truck to collect him. You're tempted to let the phone go to the message service. But your security policy insists that you answer calls, and you've been the one trying to enforce this amongst staff lately. You realise you have no choice but to answer.

You answer and hold the phone to your ear. Muffled shouting comes from the speaker. It sounds like several voices, and you hear traffic in the background.

"Hello? Michel? Is that you?"

Suddenly Michel's panicked voice comes through. "I've had a crash! I've hit someone! I've knocked them down! There's a real crowd here, they're really angry. Please come!"

"Okay, slow down, I'll come. Where are you, what's happened?"

"I'm at the edge of the market. On the road towards the river. A lady stepped out in front of me, with a baby. I hit her and the baby went flying. I think they've taken her to hospital. But the crowd here won't let me leave. I've been punched but they hit my helmet. Please hurry."

After telling Michel that you're on your way, you grab you belongings and your quick-run bag and head outside. The scooter that you use for errands is parked outside, in the shade of the tree where you left it earlier. Knowing where Michel is, you realise you will save several minutes if you go there directly, rather than riding the scooter back to your base and collecting the work pickup truck.

Do you go directly to the accident scene?

Yes: go to 1

Otherwise go to 2

1 You decide it will be quickest if you go directly to the crash site by scooter. Just before you set off, you call another colleague and ask him to bring the pickup truck to meet you there.

Ten minutes later you arrive at the market and spot Michel in the middle of a crowd of people. As you move through the crowd you catch strong whiffs of alcohol. Several of the crowd have reddened eyes. Michel spots you, and his face goes slack with relief.

"Thank you for coming. I don't know what to do. Everyone is really angry."

You hear a loud crash. You turn and see your scooter lying on the floor. Two men move away from it. It's clear they pushed it over. They look at you with anger in their eyes. Something bumps you in the back. As you turn, the man who pushed you pushes again, harder.

"Do you think these roads are a racetrack? Our children play here. You're all the same, riding your motorbikes around as if we don't exist."

You try to explain that you have just arrived and are only interested in helping the person who was hurt. Someone else further back in the crowd starts to yell at you. The noise grows.

At that moment you hear a loud engine, and the work pickup truck pulls up next to you. Your colleague steps out, and calls out a greeting to the crowd in the local dialect. To your surprise he gets a few responses. As you watch, he greets several members of the crowd, and as he does so, he subtly moves the focus of the crowd's attention away from you and Michel. You find yourself standing off to one side, as he talks with the crowd members. You watch him gesture towards the logo on the pickup's door, and then point away in what you know is the direction of the local clinic.

You take the opportunity to check with Michel if he is okay. He says he is, although he seems very shaken.

You hear your name called, and turn around. Your colleague is standing there with a policeman. "I've got this," he says. "I can stay here and fill in the accident report. You and Michel can go to the hospital to see if the family need help."

Overhearing, Michel climbs hurriedly into the truck on the passenger side. He looks very relieved to get inside the safety of the cab.

You carefully turn the truck around and pull away from the market. As you drive off, you wonder about going back to your base and waiting for things to calm down.

Do you drive straight back to your base?

Yes: go to 5

Otherwise go to 6

2 Thinking about the impression you will give if you turn up on a scooter, to a scene where a foreigner on a similar vehicle has caused an accident, you decide to fetch the work pickup truck. You're well aware of the perception that some locals have of foreigners, and you know it isn't helped by the way foreign drivers race through the city as if every call is an emergency. You decide that if you are going to try to calm the situation, you need to distance yourself from those perceptions.

You ride the scooter back to your base and exchange it for the truck. You glance around to see if any colleagues can help you, but they are all signed out on a distribution.

You drive the truck towards the market. Fifteen minutes later you arrive.

You spot Michel in the middle of a crowd of people. As you move through the crowd you catch strong whiffs of alcohol. Several of the crowd have reddened eyes. Michael spots you, and his face goes slack with relief.

"Thank you for coming. I don't know what to do. Everyone is really angry."

Do you look around for people in authority to talk to?

Yes: go to 3

Otherwise go to 4

3 You ask Michel if the police are there. He tells you that two of them came, and one went with the injured lady and baby by taxi to the hospital. He said the other is around somewhere, and has told him not to leave the accident scene.

You spot a group of older men sitting outside one of the small shops. Walking over to them, you are relieved to notice that they don't appear to have been drinking. You explain that you're trying to make sure that the lady and the baby are okay. One of them points to your truck, and says he knows your group from a medical distribution you did a few days. When he explains this to the others, one of them gets up from his chair and heads into the crowd. A moment later he's back with the policeman.

The man who recognised the truck explains to the policeman who you are. The he turns to you. "You stay in that building near the old pumping station, is that right?"

"That's right. Two gates down."

"You see?" he says to the policeman. "You know where you can find them if you need to. Why not let them go and help out at the hospital, see if they're needed?"

To your surprise, the policeman agrees. He tells you that you are free to go.

Michel tells you his bike isn't working after the accident. With the policeman's help you hastily load it up onto the back of the pickup truck, turn the truck around, and start off down the road.

Do you go to the hospital?
Yes: go to 6   Otherwise go to 5

4 You try to address the crowd, using the local greetings that you have picked up. Some people just stare at you, but to your relief you get a few replies.

You try to explain to the crowd that you want to fix the problem, at the hospital and with the police.

Several people start talking at once, and it soon becomes a shouting match. Michel gets pushed by a few people, although they keep a respectful distance from you. The hands pushing Michel get rougher. He starts to look really scared.

Pulling Michel aside, you ask him if the police are there. He tells you that two of them came, and one went with the injured lady and baby by taxi to the hospital. He said the other is around somewhere, and has told him not to leave the accident scene.

A young couple approach you. The first thing you notice is that they don't seem to have been drinking. The lady points to your truck, and says she knows your group from a medical distribution you did a few days. When she explains this to the man with her, he heads off into the crowd. A moment later he's back with the policeman.

The lady who recognised the truck explains to the policeman who you are. The she turns to you. "You stay in that building near the old pumping station, is that right?"

"That's right. Two gates down."

"You see?" she says to the policeman. "You know where you can find them if you need to. Why not let them go and help out at the hospital, see if they're needed?"

To your surprise, the policeman agrees. He tells you that you are free to go.

Michel tells you his bike isn't working after the accident. With the policeman's help you hastily load it up onto the back of the pickup truck, turn the truck around, and start off down the road.

Do you go to the hospital?

Yes: go to 6

Otherwise go to 5

5 "We're not going to the hospital," you tell Michel, as you start to drive away. "I think we're better off getting you back to base, and letting this thing calm down."

"No, we can't do that," he replies. "That baby could be really hurt. I've got to find out what's happening and see if I can help."

"Are you sure?" you ask. "If it turns out badly, you could end up getting arrested."

"They know where we live. I'll get arrested anyway if something happens. At least I need to try to help."

Noting how determined Michel is to follow up, you drive towards the hospital

Go to 6

6 You arrive at the hospital, and after making a few enquiries you find your way to the ward where the woman and her baby are being treated.

When you arrive, you find the door to the ward is closed. Outside are a policeman and a tall man you don't recognise.

Michel speaks to them both for a minute. Then he brings the tall man to meet you. The policeman remains seated, writing on a pad of paper.

"This is the guy I was telling you about in the truck. The one who calmed people down a bit when they grabbed me off my bike. He came here with the policeman to make sure the baby is okay."

You take a few minutes to thank the man for his help.

"That's alright," he says, "Your friend here chose a bad time to have an accident. Normally people would be too busy to pay much attention, but on Sunday afternoons they have nothing else to do. They just sit around drinking, waiting to see what trouble appears."

You ask him why he took the time to help.

"Don't you remember me? I was at that clinic you ran a few days ago. I was one of the ones doing the registration on the front steps. I saw you and your friend coming in and out with all your supplies. But I was sitting at a table. There were a lot of people around. You would have seen me if I was standing up," he says with a smile.

You thank him for helping Michel. "Is there any news about the injured lady and her baby?"

"Well," he says, "it's not as bad as it seems. The bike spun her round, so there wasn't too much direct impact. And the baby fell into a pile of fruit that someone was selling. Seems that she squished the fruit instead of any part of her body. Those bruises we could see turned out to be stains from the fruit. I think they're both going to be okay."

Relieved, you ask if there's anything more you should do. The tall man pauses for a moment. "This is a poor family," he tells you. "And the hospital want to keep them in for a night to make sure there are no complications. That costs money and I don't think they can afford it. Of course your friend will need to pay for their treatment right now, but officially that ends once they are assessed. The cost of staying in for the night is an extra cost. Legally he doesn't have to pay for that."

Do you offer to pay for all the costs, including any extras?

Yes: go to 7   Maybe: go to 8   Otherwise go to 9

7 You go to the hospital's finance department, explain the case, and are asked to leave a three hundred dollar deposit to cover any costs. This seems a bit high, since the costs of the emergency treatment shouldn't be more than fifty dollars, but you arrange that you will return to collect the remainder after the family has been released.

The following day you send Michel to the hospital to collect the remaining money from the deposit. He calls you from the hospital, and tells you that the family has already left, taking with them the rest of the deposit. You realise that you have no chance of getting the money back. Resignedly, you tell him to come back to work.

Go to 12

8 It seems reasonable to you to pay for any costs from the accident. However, you want to make sure you are paying for legitimate costs.

You go to the hospital's finance department, explain the case, and are asked to leave a three hundred dollar deposit to cover any costs. This seems a bit high, since the costs of the emergency treatment shouldn't be more than fifty dollars.

You point out that your organisation is well known to the hospital, since it sometimes provides medicines when the hospital's supplies run low. After some discussion you agree that you will leave a deposit to cover the cost of treatment so far, and will pay the rest when the family are released. The finance manager agrees to make an exception to the usual payment-first policy.

The next day you send Michel to pay the outstanding amount. He calls you from the hospital. He says he is with the mother and her baby, and they are both doing fine. He asks if he can use the truck to drive them home. On the way he plans to stop and buy the family a few groceries.

It occurs to you that he might be paying off his guilt.

Do you tell him to put them on a bus and come straight back?

Yes: go to 10

Otherwise go to 11

9 "I don't think you really understood," the tall man explains. "As soon as their treatment is over, this family will be out on the street. If any complications arise there could be a real problem. This lady won't know how to detect the signs of a problem until it's too late."

"It's my fault," Michel says. "I don't want anything worse to happen. I'm going to finish the police report. **Can you take my money and go and leave a deposit?"**

Yes: go to 7

Maybe go to 8

10 You tell Michel to come straight back. "Really?" he asks. "I thought we were concerned about our community relations. I know I made a mistake but I'm trying to put it right. I thought you'd be a bit more understanding."

Go to 12

11 "I think taking them back is a great idea," you tell Michel. "And I'm sure they'll really appreciate a few groceries. You know, when word of what you've done gets around their community, it will really help our image. I know it started in a bad way, but what you're doing will help bring a good outcome. We want to be associated with supporting the community, not be seen as one of these NGOs that lives in our own world."

Go to 12

12
A week has passed since Michel's motorbike accident, and things have been fairly uneventful. The only real incident during the week was when Casandra dismissed a night guard, because she heard that he had started a full-time apprenticeship during the day. You would have preferred that she checked with you first, but you are conscious of trying to develop staff in their various capacities. Guards are her responsibility, so you accept her decision.

Leaving the cool shade of the outdoor visitor waiting area, you step inside your office and rinse your empty drink mug in the small sink. As you settle back to your work, Casandra approaches and asks if she can have a word.

"We got this letter this morning. It's from the local department of labour. Ronnie's made a complaint that he was unfairly dismissed. We've been summoned to a hearing, this afternoon. Wow, they don't give much warning, do they?"

You tell her that as the current representative of the organisation, you will go to the meeting. You ask for advice from your colleagues and discover that the office is just a five minute drive away.

After a quick lunch, you gather some paperwork and leave for the labour office. The work truck is away, in use, and the only vehicle available is the new four-wheel drive that was recently delivered. Fresh from being washed by the day guard, it stands gleaming in the sun. You wonder briefly about the image this vehicle will give off. But you know the afternoon sun is at its fiercest, and you don't have too much time before the meeting.

Do you drive to the meeting?
Yes: Go to 13   Otherwise go to 14

13 You decide it's too hot to walk, and you don't want to risk being late.

As you drive into the labour office compound, you notice a smartly dressed man sitting on the building's veranda, chatting with Ronnie, the guard who was dismissed. Neither stands up as you approach. You see them looking past you at the shiny new vehicle. You greet them both politely, and after a moment's pause the well-dressed man introduces himself as the local labour official. He tells you bluntly to follow him inside.

You all sit down and the labour official explains Ronnie's case against you. He tells you that the law states you have to give a much longer warning period before such a termination. He asks if you have anything to say.

Go to 15

14 Despite the heat, you decide to walk. You really want to be careful about the image you give off, and you fear that arriving in a shiny new four-wheel drive will send the wrong message.

You start sweating almost immediately, and when you reach the labour office twenty minutes later you're soaked.

As you walk through an open gateway into the labour office compound, you notice a smartly dressed man sitting on the building's veranda, chatting with Ronnie, the guard who was dismissed. They both stand up and greet you. The well-dressed man introduces himself as the local labour official.

Gesturing you inside, the labour official offers you a bottle of water from his fridge, which you gratefully accept.

After a bit of small talk, the official asks Ronnie to explain his case. Ronnie does so, taking quite a while. At one point the official looks at his watch, and then asks Ronnie to finish quickly. He then turns to you and asks for your explanation of events.

You think about starting with a few minutes' explanation about your organisation, a sort of standard talk that you often give donors and other interested parties. But you have no idea how long the official is prepared to listen for, and you have some important points to make about the dismissal.

Do you make sure to state your case directly, to get time to cover all your points?

Yes: go to 15

Otherwise go to 16

15

You explain the case from your point of view. You try to explain that your agency encourages Ronnie to take the apprenticeship, pointing out that it will be better for him in the long run. However, you also explain that the job he was doing requires a vigilance through the night which can't be achieved if he is awake all day.

Part way through your explanation, the official cuts you off.

"It's clear cut," he says. "In this type of case, you have to give full warning." He pulls out a tattered sheaf of papers, which he tells you are the labour law. He points you to a paragraph which is very confusing. "In this type of case, the fine is three hundred dollars. I expect you to pay right now."

You point out that the procedure is very unclear, and that you don't know why you are being fined.

The administrator asks Ronnie to step outside for a moment.

"Maybe you don't understand," he says. "I could order you to pay that man two months' salary for dismissing him too quickly, as well as this fine. You should consider me a friend, only setting a minimum fine."

You decide that it is better to accept the smaller fine than to push the matter further. You explain that you have to get a receipt for any payment to the national government or to local authorities. The official pulls out a receipt book, tucks a page of blue carbon paper between two sheets, and starts to write you a receipt. The receipt has an official letterhead at the top. While the official writes, he tugs and pulls on the carbon paper, and goes over some of his writing several times. You wonder what the problem is, for his pen seems to be working fine. At one point you offer him the use of your pen, but he waves the offer away dismissively.

He tears off your copy and passes it to you, swiftly tucking his own receipt book back in the desk. You can't be certain from your quick glance, but it seemed as though his copy only had the number thirty marked in the number column, not a three and two zeroes. Before you know it, he's ushered you outside.

You say goodbye to Ronnie and head away. At the end of the road, just before you turn down a side street, you glance back. You can still make out the building, with Ronnie and the official standing in the shade of the veranda. You can't be sure due to the distance, but it seems like the official passes something to Ronnie. A passing car beeps loudly. You jump back out of the way, put the afternoon's events to the back of your mind, and turn your focus onto returning to work.

Go to 19

16

You're aware that you may not have a lot of time to make your case. But you feel it is important to make sure that the official understands who your organisation is, and how much you are invested in the welfare of the local people.

After explaining a little about your organisation, you describe the particular case. You encourage Ronnie to take the apprenticeship, pointing out that it will be better for him in the long run. Nonetheless, you also explain that the job he was doing requires a vigilance through the night which can't be achieved if he is awake all day.

The official takes a few moments to consider the case. Then he agrees with you, explaining to Ronnie that your reasoning is valid.

He then takes out a copy of the labour law, and points to a procedural error in the way that the dismissal was handled. You read the procedure; it's very unclear what your agency should have done in order to comply.

The official explains that there is a fifty dollar fine for the incorrect dismissal.

Do you protest against the fine?

Yes: go to 17

Otherwise go to 18

17
You point out that the procedure is very unclear, and that you don't know why you are being fined.

The administrator asks Ronnie to step outside for a moment.

"Maybe you don't understand," he says. "I could order you to pay that man two months' salary for dismissing him too quickly. You should consider me a friend, only setting a minimum fine."

You decide that it is better to accept the smaller fine than to push the matter further. You explain that you have to get a receipt for any payment to the national government or to local authorities. The official pulls out a receipt book, tucks a page of blue carbon paper between two sheets, and writes you a receipt. The receipt has an official letterhead at the top. While the official writes, he tugs and pulls on the carbon paper. You wonder what the problem is, for his pen seems to be working fine. At one point you offer him the use of your pen, but he waves the offer away dismissively.

He tears off your copy and passes it to you, swiftly tucking his own receipt book back in the desk. You can't be certain from your quick glance, but it seemed as though his copy only had a five marked in the number column, not a five and a zero. But before you know it, he's ushered you outside.

You say goodbye to Ronnie and walk away. At the end of the road, just before you turn down a side street, you glance back. You can still make out the building, with Ronnie and the official standing in the shade of the veranda. You can't be sure due to the distance, but it seems like the official passes something to Ronnie. A passing car beeps loudly. You step back out of the way, put the afternoon's events to the back of your mind, and turn your focus onto returning to work.
Go to 19

18

You decide that you'll accept the fine, for any further complications will only end up costing you more.

You ask him for a copy of the labour law to keep at the office. He digs around in the cabinets behind him until he finds a spare copy. He points out the relevant page and marks it with a paperclip.

As you start the hot walk back to your office you make a mental note to tell Casandra to check with you in the future before making any more quick decisions on staff dismissal.

Go to 19

19

You're at the Ministry of NGO Affairs. A requirement of the current crisis is that every relief organisation has to file a project plan every six months. Although you could send a colleague to do it, you're keen to keep your connections within the ministry. You know how helpful these connections have been in the past.

In addition, by making the submission in person you can sign the finished form directly. The alternative is a minimum of two visits by a colleague – one to collect the paperwork – if copies are available – and another to return the signed documents. The whole process usually ends up taking three or four visits and using up many hours of staff time. Right now your staff are stretched to the limit with all the distributions, and it's hard to know who to spare. You're hoping that your good connections will speed up the process considerably.

The deputy minister is in her office. She smiles as you knock and enter. You explain why you're there.

"No problem," she says. "We've seen the results of your projects. You seem to be doing all that you promised to."

"In fact," she continues, "you don't need to fill out fresh forms. I'm sure you're all busy. We can just run the previous submission through the photocopier, and you sign it with the new date." She reaches to the shelf beside her desk, pulls down a thick ring binder folder, and starts leafing through the contents, looking for your file.

You're relieved; this should save you more than two hours of form-filling.

"By the way," the deputy minister says, glancing up, "my niece just finished her college course in administration. I see you employ quite a few local staff. Do you think there could be a job for her with your group? She's very competent."

You remember a friend telling you about all the problems he had when he hired someone just to keep their relative – who was in a position of power – supportive of his agency. At the time he warned you how common the request was, since people perceived NGOs as being wealthy and being able to create as many jobs as they wanted.

Do you explain firmly to the deputy minister that this isn't the way you hire people?

Yes: go to 20

Otherwise go to 23

20

You start to explain to the deputy minister that this isn't the way that your organisation hires people.

"I see. Well, as you say, procedures are important. Maybe I shouldn't be breaking procedure with your paperwork. It might be better if you fill in a fresh copy. Oh, and I've remembered the new procedure where we require audited accounts with every submission. I think we had better honour procedures and ask for that too."

Inwardly you groan. What she's asking for will take many hours to complete.

Do you suggest you might have work for her niece after all?

Yes: go to 21   **Otherwise go to 22**

21

Thinking how important it is to have good relations with those in positions of power, you explain that maybe there's a place for her niece at your work after all.

"Well, that's really thoughtful of you," says the deputy director. "Let's see what we can do about this paperwork." She calls her secretary and instructs her to make copies of your report.

When you return to the office and tell your colleagues that a new staff member is joining you, there's a lot of surprise. Once you explain the background, a few of your more experienced staff nod resignedly. You realise that for the newer staff it will take a lot more explaining.

Ends.

22 You realise that no matter the delay, you simply can't afford to take on staff as a favour to people in positions of influence.

You politely explain that you simply don't have work available at the moment.

The deputy director looks at you. "I thought your organisation had lots of work. Well, when I get your full audited report I imagine I'll understand a lot better. I hope you realise it's due by the end of the week. If I don't have it I can't authorise you to keep operating, that's the law."

You realise that you are looking at some very late nights in order to get the paperwork completed in time. As you head back to your office you console yourself by thinking that at least you won't be dealing with an unwanted staff member. Nonetheless you regret the change to your relationship with the deputy minister, and wonder how long it will take to get things back to how they were.

Ends.

23
You've learned from other encounters in the culture that a blunt "no" can be offensive to people. You look for other ways to redirect the question.

Do you ask the deputy minister if she has a CV for her niece?

Yes: go to 24

Maybe: go to 25

Otherwise go to 26

24
You ask for a CV, explaining that you have a clear and documented recruitment process, which you have registered with the Ministry of Labour. You take a moment to explain the process.

The deputy minister tells you that she doesn't have a CV with her, so you give her a business card and ask the niece to send an electronic copy to your office. You explain that you will keep the CV on file, and next time there is a job which fits her skills you will include her on the list of people to interview.

The deputy minister thanks you for taking an interest in her family. She finds your file amongst the paperwork, calls out to her secretary, and instructs her to photocopy the file.

"That should only take a few minutes. Once she's finished you can sign it. I'll stamp it and you'll be done."

As you thank her, you calculate that you've probably saved over twenty hours of staff time in the whole process.

Ends.

25 You explain that you don't have any open jobs for administrators at this point. However you ask for a CV, explaining that you have a clear and documented recruitment process, which you have registered with the Ministry of Labour. You take a moment to explain the process.

The deputy minister tells you that she doesn't have a CV with her, so you give her a business card and ask the niece to send an electronic copy to your office. You explain that you will keep the CV on file, and next time there is a job which fits her skills you will include her on the list of people to interview.

The deputy minister thanks you for taking an interest in her family. She finds your file amongst the paperwork, calls out to her secretary, and instructs her to photocopy the file.

"That should only take a few minutes. Once she's finished you can sign it. I'll stamp it and you'll be done."

As you thank her, you calculate that you've probably saved over twenty hours of staff time in the whole process.

Ends.

26 There's a long pause. The deputy minister holds your gaze. You start to feel uncomfortable.

Do you offer her niece a job?

Yes: go to 21

Otherwise go to 20

Perceptions

The first chapter in this book considered the role of values in guiding decision making. The more you recognise, understand, and can balance values, the more effectively you will make decisions under pressure.

Values are also affected by the way in which you perceive yourself. If you perceive yourself as a caring person, you will try to act in a caring way when you face a situation of need. And if you act in a caring way when you encounter a situation of need, this will reinforce your self-perception that you are a caring person. Ultimately, the way you perceive yourself has an effect on the way in which you make decisions.

Disaster response situations move you beyond self-perception. They also involve the perceptions that others have of you. In a cross-cultural situation, you will interact with many people, all of whom will have their own perception of you. Sometimes these perceptions will be favourable but you will often be following on from the earlier, less helpful activities of others. There is a very real risk that your own actions will be limited by others' pre-conceived perceptions of who you are.

There will be many situations where you enter with the best of intentions. In spite of this, the actions of your predecessors, of other humanitarian workers, and of other foreigners in general – combined with any prejudices found in the society you are entering – will result in you being perceived very differently to your own self-perception.

Your self-perception – tied in to your values – might be that you are a person sacrificing a comfortable life, family, and a good career, taking a pay cut, living in a new level of hardship, all in order to help people who are going through a huge calamity.

To the onlooker, however, you may be perceived as someone making a good salary out of other people's misery, saving money by amassing expensive per-diems, living a life of comfort in an all-inclusive hotel complex, driving an expensive, air conditioned four wheel drive, holding a position that you're far too inexperienced to justify, and regularly leaving your national colleagues while you take exotic holidays as recuperation breaks. Furthermore, the onlooker's perception, if they have seen many relief workers come and leave, is that you will only be in their country for a few weeks or months, and that you have no understanding of their lives or the situation.

No matter how well-intentioned you are, and however 'pure' your values are, the way others perceive your intentions will often be very different from your self-perception.

Understanding perceptions

Part of responding well in a situation is managing the perception of others. But how can you know how you are perceived? This can be hard enough in your own culture. When thrown into a new environment, in a culture very different to your own, it becomes so much harder.

The starting point is to think about the image you portray to others. Where are you staying? What type of vehicle are you driving? What kind of furniture is in your office? Do you have simple fans or a fully air-conditioned office? What level of wealth do you display – as shown by the venue where you take your meals, in the quality of technology you display, in the clothing you wear?

What kind of relationships do you have – do you emphasise your friendship with other foreign workers, or do you take time to form local friendships? Do you know the names of all your colleagues, even those who do less prestigious work? Do you take time to help colleagues with their work and personal challenges – or do you focus on your own work?

Essentially this starting point involves looking at your own presence and your actions and considering how they may be perceived.

The next step is to apply this reflective thinking to your overall organisation. Does your organisation lock itself away in a fortress-like compound, with high walls, razor wire and armed guards? Does it have offices which seem secretive and inaccessible to a local resident? Do neighbours understand the organisation's purpose for being there? Are local people suspicious about your activities, or do they have some understanding of what you do?

A third step is to try to understand how you and your organisation are perceived, when it comes to your role in the community. For example, are you perceived as a rich foreign company, holding back on goodwill? The thinking may be along the lines of "You have lots of money. You have lots of work positions. You could choose to make my family prosper too if you wanted, by giving us a job."

All of this requires time and insight. It would be easy to dismiss it during the pressure that comes with responding to a sudden disaster. However, in the majority of cases disaster response projects are measured in weeks and months, not days. Even in the most acute emergencies, there are points of less activity. These points may occur when waiting for transport, or for the delivery of a shipment of goods, or simply when breaking for a drink or meal. These are ideal points to try to ask some of the questions listed above, either through self-reflection, or in conversation with others.

Overcoming unhelpful perceptions

Chapter two suggested that one key step in making quick, high quality decisions under pressure is to develop the 'structure for spontaneity.' By knowing your own values – your self-perceptions – and creating a hierarchy of values, you are more easily able to respond rapidly to a situation of value conflict.

The perceptions of others also have an impact on your level of effectiveness. Where your actions are misunderstood or resented it can cause people to impose unhelpful obstacles to your work. When it comes to these perceptions, you can improve the decision-making environment if you actively focus on improving the way that you and your organisation are viewed. Recognise that you are probably starting from a position of being poorly perceived, and aim to overcome this. As you do so, you will create a more favourable environment in which to operate.

Improving the way you are perceived, as an individual and an organisation, is an ongoing task. It requires a concerted focus and deliberate action. It also depends on your level of influence within the organisation. Clearly some roles have a greater potential than others when it comes to influencing the organisation's overall approach. Yet you can make small improvements, no matter what role you hold.

For example, how does your organisation drive in the streets around your office? Are you a threat to children playing on the street, as you rush from task to task? If your role includes driving, you can commit to driving in a slower, safer manner. If your organisation employs drivers, you may be in a position to specify driving standards – and then enforce them. If you are a passenger without an authority role, you can still talk to a driver and ask them to drive more reasonably. If behaviour doesn't change, you can take it up with the driver's manager. The act of improving driving standards has two beneficial consequences. Firstly, it reduces the likelihood of accidents occurring, which in turn precludes you from having to make decisions about an accident. Secondly, it improves people's perceptions of you, which means that if an incident occurs, you are more likely to find favourable support in the community.

Issues such as the way you drive may be small individually, but cumulatively these issues add up and can improve people's perception of you and your organisation. By improving these perceptions you are improving the likelihood that 'spontaneous' favourable outcomes will present themselves at decision points.

Other points to consider for improving outside perceptions of you and your organisation include:

1. Treat each person that you encounter with dignity, whether that is the local street sweeper, the shopkeeper, or the gate guard at a large organisation.

2. When you have the possibility to help someone, help them. Within the bounds of good security practices, always be on the lookout for people to help. This is especially important in your own neighbourhood or areas that you frequent. If your organisation has a vehicle in an area with limited transport, look to provide people with lifts wherever possible.

3. Don't limit your kindness or politeness to those that you think are important, or useful to your work.

4. Learn the local greetings and the words for 'thank you.' Even if you can only start the first sentence of the conversation in the local language, it can go a long way in a tense situation. If there are terms of respect in a culture, for example when addressing older people, try to learn and use these too.

5. Learn names wherever possible. Examples include local shopkeepers and the staff at other organisations where you often have work. Try to notice those that others generally overlook such as guards or reception staff.

6. Pay attention to the way you dress. Try to avoid anything that will cause unnecessary offence in the culture or that will cause others to take you less seriously. For men, this may include wearing long trousers even in hot weather, or a polo or short-sleeved shirt rather than a t-shirt. For women, this may involve dressing more modestly than in many Western countries. Do not base your standards of dress on a country's international areas such as airports and upmarket malls, but by the areas that you visit away from these centres of wealth.

7. Aim to limit how much wealth you have on display. Many disasters affect poor areas disproportionately, and the trappings of wealth that are common in the cities of these countries may not be so present in poorer areas.

8. Be discreet if you are going to break local customs. For example, if drinking alcohol in a country where it is

generally not consumed, find ways to limit how openly you do so.

9. Be patient. Even in the rush of responding to a disaster, many cultures approach time differently to the average international aid organisation. Use 'buffer days' of waiting for equipment or transport as a chance to get to know local colleagues and to start to build trust.

Perceptions:
Principles to remember

CHAPTER SEVEN

OTHER ORGANISATIONS

Operating in a disaster response environment usually involves interaction with other responders. The types of responders you may encounter include local community-based organisations (CBOs), international non-governmental organisations (NGOs), United Nations (UN) agencies, government agencies, and private individuals and companies.

The decisions that you make in disaster response will often be made under conditions of pressure. This pressure may come from having a limited window of time to complete an action, or from security threats within the operating environment. It may come from team members with different views on how to solve a problem or from the self-interest of different local groups. In addition, the pressure at the decision point sometimes comes from other responding agencies. Understanding the types of pressure that other responders contribute to a situation, and having strategies for dealing with it, are essential components of making effective decisions.

Scenario Seven

The nights at the mountain transit camp (Scenario Five) have blurred into each other. Winter has arrived, and snowfalls are no longer an occasional occurrence; they now hit day and night with little warning.

The local police have responded in force since the first crowd surge, and they now have high, reinforced fences in place. They have boosted their numbers too, and a heavy cordon now runs from the transit site for quite a distance along the mountain track.

With the refugee crisis growing, many agencies' budgets are stretched, and supplies at the camp are running low. You've been grateful for the help of a café in the local town which has been providing large vats of hot soup at cost price, saying it is their way of caring for those in need. They had asked your staff to distribute the soup, explaining that none of their people can work at night due to the needs of the business during the day. The soup is gratefully received by those passing through, and you know it has played a role in keeping many from feeling harsher effects from the cold.

In the middle of the night a young man approaches your food tent. You recognise him from a coordination meeting. His agency vest is stretched tight over a large dark duffel jacket. His headlight blinds you and you have to ask him to point it down.

He tells you that he was at a national coordination meeting during the day, and that the local commissioner insisted that all food should come through the commissioner's office. He informs you that based on what the commissioner said, you should stop serving food.

Beside him, in the food queue, people stand shivering, waiting for him to step aside. You look back into the food tent. As well as the soup which is reheating on a gas burner, there are over fifty litres more on standby in large, insulated flasks.

Do you disregard his suggestions and carry on serving soup?

Yes: go to 1

Maybe: go to 2

Otherwise go to 3

1 You thank him for passing on the message. However, you explain that for such a serious issue as this you will need to hear directly from the commissioner. In the meantime, the humanitarian imperative to save lives compels you to keep sharing hot soup on such a cold night.

He mutters something about agencies that make it harder for everyone by running their own shows. Then he walks back along the track and out of sight.

Go to 4

2

Do you explain to him that you will make a point of seeing the commissioner in the morning, but that you will carry on serving the soup that is there?

Yes: Go to 1   Otherwise go to 3

3

You tell your team to stop serving the hot soup.

"Stop serving? But these people are freezing. What do we do, let the soup go to waste?"

You try to explain to your team that there is a new directive from the commissioner.

"Maybe. But the commissioner's not here right now. Look at these people, they need help. Surely you can see that."

In many ways you agree with your team. But you don't want to go against the commissioner's instructions. You call out to the queue that due to government control, you are no longer giving out soup. A chorus of upset voices rings out from the crowd.

"There's still tea," you call out to people. For the next few minutes, the faces that appear at the front of the queue are sullen and angry. Several people point to the vat of soup that lies cooling on the boiler.

You find it very hard to look people in the eye, as you instruct people to move the containers of soup to the back of the tent.

Go to 4

4 Later that night the temperature hits a new low. The transit stop normally has a good supply of blankets, but due to the high demand they have all been given out. As you walk through the bottlenecked crowd, you spot many shivering children. To your surprise, the adults with them have no blankets.

"Where is your blanket?" you ask one, using gestures to point to the blanket on his child.

A man steps forward from the crowd. "They gave their blankets to their children," he says. "The blanket tent was only giving out one blanket per adult. They wouldn't give them to children."

You're exasperated. On several occasions you had told the blanket tent to start cutting their blankets down into more manageable sizes. You have explained to them how this will ensure there are more blankets to go around. But the supply manager always said he was following instructions, and that he should just give out blankets as they are, one per adult. You're frustrated at his lack of initiative and inability to adjust his plans to the situation, but you realise you need to focus on finding a solution.

You remember that one of the cleaners had been going round at the start of the night shift, collecting discarded blankets from the temporary sheds where they had been used overnight and then abandoned by families making the daytime trek. You think you know where she went with the blankets she had collected.

Calling a colleague to go with you, you head for the large staff tent. Near the back, behind a small mound of mattresses, is a huge pile of recycled blankets. You and your colleague scoop up as many as you can carry, and head out of the staff tent.

As you reach the door, an off-duty NGO worker stands up.

"We were told those can't be re-used," he says. "They have to be trashed. Although I think one of the cleaners is going to take them home and wash them and use them herself."

You ask him what he means about them not being useable.

"There's been some cases of scabies reported at the next border. Apparently reusing the blankets could cause more cases to develop. Our agency had strict instructions from the national health cluster."

Do you continue to take the blankets?

Yes; go to 5

Maybe: go to 6

Otherwise go to 8

5 You take a moment and explain to him the building threat of violence from people if they get too cold.

"You're new, so you won't have experienced it," you tell him, "but a while back we had a riot when people took things into their own hands. I agree, the scabies is a problem, but scabies won't cause people to riot. Feeling like they're going to die of cold if they don't do something will."

You motion to your colleague, and step out of the tent with the blankets. You head into the crowd and distribute the extra blankets. People take them eagerly, and you find yourself making several trips until all the blankets are used. The man who spoke to you about the blankets sits sullenly in the NGO tent. He ignores your request to help with the distribution.

The night passes without incident, and you feel pleased that there was no repeat of the earlier crowd surge. As you are leaving at the end of your shift, you spot the cleaner who had collected the blankets.

"I'm sorry," you tell her. "I know you were going to take those blankets home. But we really needed them last night."

"That's okay," she replies. "I was only taking them because I thought they were going to be thrown out. If they helped keep some people warm, I'm quite happy with that."

Seeing an opportunity, you ask her if she can take any blankets she collects in the day to your food tent, rather than the large staff tent. That way, you know your team will have them on hand if supplies run low again.

She agrees, and you join your team for the ride back to the motel.

Later that afternoon you get a phone call from your regional manager. She says they've received a complaint from the coordinator of the national health cluster. You explain your reasoning, but she takes a lot of convincing. Finally she tells you to continue with what you are doing, but to try to remember that the organisation needs to work in a spirit of cooperation with others – not just for this crisis but for the future. You end the call, and realise that over an hour of your valuable time before the next shift has just been used up.

Go to 9

6 You take a moment and explain to him the building threat of violence from people if they get too cold.

"You're new, so you won't have experienced it," you tell him, "but a while back we had a riot when people took things into their own hands. I agree, the scabies is a problem, but scabies won't cause people to riot. Feeling like they're going to die of cold if they don't do something will."

"If it's a concern to you," you carry on, "we'll make sure these are distributed well away from your agency's tents. That way no-one can accuse you of being part of it."

He still seems fairly hesitant.

Do you carry on with the blankets?

Yes: go to 7   **Otherwise go to 8**

7 You explain that you will keep the distribution well away from his agency's tent, and if anyone asks, you'll take full responsibility for the decision.

You motion to your colleague, and step out of the tent with the blankets. You head into the crowd and put a pile down in a space beside the track. People take them eagerly, and you find yourself making several trips until all the blankets are used. The man who spoke to you about the blankets joins you in the distribution.

"I appreciate you keeping these away from our place," he says. "But I can see that they're really needed. There's a laundromat in town. Maybe we can set up a washing programme. These are too good to go to waste. I'll talk to my manager about it tomorrow."

The night passes without incident, and you feel pleased that there was no repeat of the earlier crowd surge. As you are leaving at the end of your shift, you spot the cleaner who had collected the blankets.

"I'm sorry," you tell her. "I know you were going to take those blankets home. But we really needed them last night."

"That's okay," she replies. "I was only taking them because I thought they were going to be thrown out. If they helped keep some people warm, I'm quite happy with that." Seeing an opportunity, you ask her if she can take any blankets she collects in the day to your food tent, rather than the large staff tent. That way, you know your team will have them on hand if supplies run low again. She agrees, and you join your team for the ride back to the motel.

Go to 9

8 You think about what you've been told. You don't want to cause a spread of disease, and you don't want to go against the directive from the health cluster.

You tell your colleague that you will have to leave it. He looks at you in surprise, but follows your guidance. After several night shifts, you suspect he is too tired to argue.

You both walk outside and head back to the food tent. Shortly after, as you're heating up a fresh batch of tea, you start to hear shouting. A moment later a rush of people push past the tent entrance. They're followed by another surge, and this group push up against the food tent. You hear shouts of pain and confusion.

"It's another surge!" someone shouts. Two bodies stumble against the outside of the tent. They knock the large pot of tea towards you, and the hot liquid spills onto your arm. Flames from the gas cooker shoot up. Blocking out the pain in your arm, you desperately reach for the gas valve.

As you step outside, the surge comes back up the track, like a receding wave. Worried-looking people stumble backwards. Soon afterwards a line of police push their way through the tent alley, wooden sticks swinging harshly at anyone who won't retreat.

For the rest of the night, the camp is filled with an uneasy tension. You spend a long time making sure that your team are unharmed before you're able to finally get some treatment for your burned arm.

Go to 9

9 The track out of the transit area has become increasingly churned up. You know that families were able to get wheelchairs through earlier in the year. But with the snow, ice and rain, many areas have turned to thick mud. Now, faced with two families with wheelchair-bound members, you realise the situation is different.

One family had been sheltering in the clinic, the daughter getting treated for mild frostbite after a trip along the track ended in near-disaster. She and her family were brought back by a very unselfish group of young men, who risked further aggression from the police by returning. One of them explained as he left that there was no way they could carry the patient through on the track, since they had to keep up with the rest of the people from their village. They only brought her because she and her family were so near the start of the journey.

The other family has joined, being drawn to the first family as a source of information about the journey. It's clear to them that if a light girl in a wheelchair can't get through, then there's no way that the overweight, war-wounded brother in their group could make it. The clinic has asked them all to leave to make room for others, so they're sheltering together in one of the plastic housing sheds.

You've been working on their problem for a couple of hours now. Finally, one of your colleagues comes in. She has a reputation for being a real go-getter, and has the most 'can-do' attitude you've ever come across.

"I found a farmer partway down the mountain. He's rented me his quad bike and trailer. It's really strong. We should have no problem getting through the mountain pass on it. In fact, I think we need to get onto our donors to see if we can buy one of these. It's going to be really essential in the coming months."

Do you help the disabled people onto the trailer and send them on the journey?

Yes: go to 10

Maybe: go to 11

Otherwise go to 12

10

You help the disabled people onto the trailer, tying their wheelchairs down at the back. Each of them is joined by a relative. Covering them all with blankets and a tarpaulin, you tell your colleague to drive carefully.

As they drive off they wave in gratitude. One of the families thanks your team, and they walk off behind the quad bike.

Four hours later, you're beginning to get worried. Your colleague should be back by now. Calling another colleague to join you, you pack a small bag each and prepare to head off down the track to check on her. You hang your agency badges clearly around your neck, hoping to avoid any trouble with the police at the barriers.

After walking half an hour you see your colleague coming towards you.

"We got stopped," she says. "They wanted to arrest me for people trafficking! Can you believe it? I got those patients to the bus park, thankfully. But they confiscated the quad bike. They said it was being used for people trafficking. I have to go back there in the morning with the farmer, to prove that it's his. I'm not sure how I'm going to break the news to him. He's going to be furious."

You're glad that she's okay. But you can just picture all the trouble you're going to have getting the quad bike back. There goes today's sleep, you think ruefully.

Go to 15

11 "I think we'd better hold on a moment," you tell your colleague. "Don't Disability Alliance have some of their people here? I know they don't do the night shift, but I think I saw a couple of people sleeping in the staff tent. Maybe they've decided to wait here between shifts rather than go back to town. We could ask them for a cover letter."

You walk over to the staff tent. Two of the Disability Alliance staff lie huddled on green army sleeping cots, buried under several blankets. You wake one and explain the situation. Sleepily, he explains that if you're stopped, you should say that DA gave you permission to transport the people, since they have a universal clearance to move people.

You're a bit concerned about the language barrier with the police and soldiers who line the route.

Do you tell your colleague to go ahead, using the verbal assurances from Disability Alliance?

Yes: Go to 10

Maybe: Go to 12

Otherwise go to 14

12
You're really concerned about the risk of the police treating your colleague as a people smuggler.

You start to explain this to her. She points out how important it is to help

The lady from Disability Alliance comes into the tent where your discussing the issue.

"I heard what's going on," she says. "You know, we're not allowed to work during the night shift for security reasons. But I can get you a cover letter from our tent. It's the general form we use when transporting patients. That should work fine, if I write your name on it and you carry agency ID."

Do you let your colleague go, using the cover letter?

Yes: Go to 13

Otherwise go to 14

13

You help the disabled people onto the trailer, tying their wheelchairs down at the back. Each of them is joined by a relative. Covering them all with blankets and a tarpaulin, you tell your colleague to drive carefully.

As they drive off they wave in gratitude. One of the families thanks your team, and they walk off behind the quad bike.

Three hours later, your colleague returns. She looks tired but exhilarated. "We have got to get one of these," she says, pointing to the quad bike. "There's no way a wheelchair would make it through there. We could help so many people if we had a quad bike. Do you think we can rent this a bit longer from the farmer? And I can write a proposal this afternoon, to see if we can get some funding."

As you settle back to other tasks, you feel pleased with the outcome. And you realise that your team have stumbled on an area of significant need that you can meet. You decide to help your colleague with her funding proposal that afternoon.

Go to 15

14

You weigh up the risks of transporting people. You know the police are very strict right now, and the last thing you want is for your staff to be detained and your agency name put in a bad light.

"It's not going to work," you tell your colleagues. "It's just too risky. We have no guarantees that we'll be permitted to carry people. You could easily be arrested for people smuggling."

Your colleague is very disappointed. She tries to explain that she made so much effort to get the quad bike as transport, and that the family have little other option.

While you discuss the issue, a crowd builds in the small resting tent. You work out that they must be from the same town as the people you are trying to help. After a lot of discussion some young men step forward. One of them picks up the young disabled girl. Four other grab the corners of a stretcher that they've made from some thick scaffolding poles and some extra jackets. Hoisting the disabled man on it, they work their way through the doorway and head off.

You and your colleagues step outside and watch them walk off into the distance. You wonder if they have any chance of succeeding.

Go to 15

15 Two days have gone by without a major incident up on the mountain. However, there have been worrying reports of relief workers being threatened by security forces at the mountain camp. Your own team has a maintained a good relationship with the local police. A few days ago a police car had run its battery flat, and your team gave a jump start using your booster cables, getting them going again. In the process you met the local police captain, and you have made a point of visiting him when you work at the camp.

You have a large minibus which you use to transport your people between your motel base in town and the mountain transit site. As you often have spare seats you have committed to providing another relief agency, People In Crisis, with transport for their team too. Their own van is at a local garage being repaired. You are usually joined by about six members from PIC.

As evening comes you pull on several layers of warm clothing and walk out to the motel car park, ready to take the minibus up the mountain. Your phone rings, and you see it is your colleague who is leading the day shift.

"Hi Jacques, we're about to leave. We'll be with you soon."

"No, it's not that. Listen, there's been a disturbance. This really agitated group of locals came through and some trouble broke out with the police. We're all safe because the group ran off down the road towards the city. But the police have gone after them, and we can hear a lot of noise from further down the road. We're all safe to stay here for a while and keep working. I mean, we're tired, and those two new volunteers got quite scared. Also, we're low on supplies and need what you have in the minibus. But if you drive up here now you'll be driving right through the trouble."

You explain this to the group that's gathered round you – your own team and the night shift from PIC. You mention that you may delay going up the mountain.

One of the PIC staff objects. "We've had these reports before," he says. "Last week we were told there was trouble from a local group. But when they saw our NGO vehicle they left us alone."

Do you trust your status as an NGO, and drive up the mountain, through potential trouble, to the camp?

Yes: go to 16

Maybe: go to 17

Otherwise go to 19

16

Deciding to trust your status as an NGO, you all get in the minibus and start the drive up the mountain. Most of the drive passes without incident, and you're only a few minutes away from the transit camp. The minibus slows, and navigates a narrow bend through a rocky area.

Suddenly, as you come through the bend, you find yourself at the back of a large crowd. They fill the road, carrying sticks, bats, and tyre levers. Through a gap in the crowd, not far away, you see a wide line of police, advancing towards you. The crowd surge past the minibus, shouting. Hands and weapons crash against the bus as they pass. You hear a loud crash, and the side window shatters. Your colleague shouts in fright.

A few moments later the police are upon you. They yell at you to get out of the way. One of them thrusts a baton through the driver's window, right into your face. His message is clear – get the bus out of there.

As quickly as possible, you edge past the police and up the mountain road. When you reach the camp you stop and check your passengers. Most look shaken, and one of the People In Crisis volunteers is crying quietly. You get out and check the minibus. Two windows are broken, the side mirrors have been ripped off and hang limply by their connecting cables, and the bodywork is dented in many places.

You inform the afternoon shift that they will need to wait for another two hours before returning to the town, to make sure that the riot has died down.

Ends.

17

You are concerned about the risk of driving into a violent situation. You are not sure that you agree with the staff of People In Crisis about how you will be safe just because you are an NGO.

Your colleague mentions that one day there was a flood on the mountain, closing the road at a small river ford. At that time, he tells you, they took a different route up the mountain. He says it took them an extra two hours, and that some of the journey felt quite scary, with long drops in some places beside the narrow road. He says they made the journey during the day and he hasn't tried it at night. He remembers there were several forks in the road where they almost got lost. However, he says that with a good driver it should be okay.

Do you take the longer route instead?

Yes: go to 18

Otherwise go to 19

18 You decide to take the longer route. Since you are a bit tired, you ask your colleague to drive. You trust her driving, and you know that she is fresh after having a few days' break in the main city.

The journey goes slowly, and at some points you are grateful for the darkness, so that you can't see how far the drop at the edge of the road is.

Eventually you reach the camp. You find your colleagues and together you unload the new supplies. You advise them to spend the night in the staff tent rather than run the risk of the dangerous mountain road again. Also, you can't be sure if the riot is clear and you don't want them driving down the main road and into potential trouble.

That night the camp is busy as refugees pass through, and you are glad for the extra supplies that you brought.

Ends.

19 You remember that you have the number of the police captain. You wonder if he could give you any advice about the current situation. But you don't want to hurt the good relationship by disturbing him, if he is in the middle of dealing with a riot situation.

Do you call him for advice?

Yes: go to 20　　　　**Otherwise go to 22**

20

You call the number you have for the police captain.

"Oh, yes," he says, "it's good to hear from you. It's a good idea to call. Actually, that road is not safe. My men are still there. Most of the trouble is over but still there are a few troublemakers."

"So you think we should avoid the road for now?" you ask.

"Well, I know you're doing good work up here. I have some of my men in town right now. They are getting us more supplies. If you want, one of them can come back up the mountain with you. That way, I don't think you'll have any problems."

You tell him you will think about it for a minute, and call him back if you need a policeman to go with you. You mention it to the others. The staff at People In Crisis are a bit concerned about the image that it gives off. However, they acknowledge that it is in your vehicle, not theirs, so they accept that it is not their decision.

Do you make the journey up the mountain, using a police escort?

Yes: go to 21

Otherwise go to 22

21 You reason that if you have a police escort, that you can safely make the journey. After calling the captain to accept his support, you tell your team and the staff from People In Crisis that you will go up to the camp.

Stopping first in the town centre to collect a policeman, you make the drive up the mountain. At one point the policeman tells you to pull over, as his phone has picked up a signal. He makes a quick phone call, then tells you to proceed.

You arrive at the camp without incident, although you can tell from the drive in that there has been a lot of agitation. Several parked cars have broken windows and damage to the bodywork. Broken glass lines the street and a few tyres lie smouldering in small piles. At one point you glance up a steep side street and see a large group of police lining the road. Through your open window you hear a lot of chanting in the distance. The policeman taps you on the shoulder and tells you to keep driving.

As you pull into the camp you notice that you get a few glances from other aid workers. You can't tell if they are surprised to see a policeman in your vehicle, or if they are just surprised to see any vehicles on the main road given the recent riot.

You find your colleagues from the afternoon shift and together you unload the new supplies. You advise them to spend the night in the staff tent rather than run the risk of driving down the road. You can't be sure if the riot is clear and you don't want them driving down the main road and into potential trouble.

That night the camp is busy as refugees pass through, and you are glad for the extra supplies that you brought.   **Ends.**

22 You decide that there are too many risks building up. You don't want to run the risk of possibly driving into a riot, and the possible injury to your colleagues or damage to your vehicle. You also worry about the image you will give off by involving the police.

You tell your colleagues that regretfully you will not be travelling at this time, and that you will wait for an update from the transit camp security manager.

Your own staff accept the decision and return to their rooms. You are about to call your colleagues up on the mountain to advise them of the decision when the leader of the People In Crisis team approaches you.

"We're really unhappy about this. We were relying on you to help us do our job. Now those refugees up there aren't going to get the support they need tonight."

You explain that your primary concern is your own staff, not People In Crisis's programming. Before you can explain more, the leader walks away. You hear him on the phone to a taxi firm, calling for a taxi. A few minutes later a taxi pulls into the motel car park and the People In Crisis team squeeze in.

The next morning you go to a security briefing about the night's riot, organised by one of the bigger NGOs. They give details of what happened and make some recommendations for the future. Then someone in the meeting mentions that they just had a call from the hospital. It seems that some People In Crisis staff, in a taxi, had driven into the middle of the riot last night. The taxi driver and one of the PIC passengers are in hospital being treated for quite severe injuries. **Ends.**

Other organisations

In many situations of disaster response, particularly in large-scale responses, it is common to find yourself operating alongside other organisations. This may be at a project site, where you find yourself delivering foodstuffs next to a group which is running a child-friendly space. It may be at a coordination meeting where you encounter groups with similar agendas to your own.

Often the majority of NGOs in a situation will follow a particular approach. This may be in regards to which local authority to deal with, or in the type of support that is best for the situation. It may be to do with a commonly-followed security standard. In such situations it can be easy for the favoured approach to gain traction as the 'right' way to deal with a problem. Where this happens it can be common to find a level of peer pressure developing. NGOs and their staff who propose alternative approaches may be viewed as less competent.

In these situations the temptation is to let a 'standard' NGO approach guide your decision making. In order to make decisions well, it is important to avoid falling into the trap of accepting the prevailing view without question. To avoid this trap, try to bear in mind a few key points.

Firstly, don't assume the standard NGO position on a topic is the wisest one. Don't assume that other organisations can see the big picture. These organisations may be driven by donor pressure to follow a particular course of action. They may be driven by bureaucratic pressure to follow the guidance of a particular ministry or department. They may be run by inexperienced managers who don't have sufficient exposure to the longer-term effects of different actions.

Disaster response organisations are often staffed by people who don't really understand the local culture or context. They may have rushed in from another disaster situation, and lack background understanding. Their organisations might have good response systems but those systems may not be the best fit for every situation.

If possible, try to find the experienced people in the situation. In a coordination meeting, for example, this may be the cluster coordinator. But it is equally likely to be a different member in the room. Coordinators change, and in the rapid turnover of personnel that is a feature of disaster response the person leading the meeting may be newly arrived. Some of the other people in the room may have a much better understanding of the situation. Finding the most knowledgeable person may involve identifying people who have been in a location well before the disaster, or who have responded elsewhere in the same country on previous occasions. Listen carefully when different members of a coordination meeting speak, and try to identify who really knows what they are talking about.

Once you have identified the real people of knowledge, try to learn from their guidance. Make a point of meeting them and asking for a few minutes of their time. Ask about longer-term trends, or potentially harmful activities. When making decisions, let their guidance influence you more than the 'conventional wisdom' in the room.

Dynamic, fast-changing conditions

After a disaster, conditions can change rapidly and often. A response which was appropriate at one point becomes obsolete as people move, security levels fluctuate or government directives change. This means that a rule, regulation, or instruction which was once valid may quickly become obsolete.

In making decisions it is important to recognise the dynamic, changeable nature of the situation. A statement or a rule might be static, and therefore no longer relevant to your decision. Consider the following example: in the early days of a response following a large-scale disaster, a local authority insists that all fresh food donations to a camp are delivered from that authority's on-site feeding kitchen. Any organisation attempting to deliver food directly to people in the camp would be told to direct the food to the local authority's kitchen module. However, in the weeks that follow, the national Ministry of Health issues a temporary licence to certain organisations to deliver their own food directly. The operating environment and the process of delivering food are dynamic entities. The static instruction to deliver through the local authority becomes outdated.

In the example above, making a decision about where and how to deliver food requires an up-to-date knowledge of the situation. If the decision maker relies on the guidance of minutes from a cluster meeting, or the advice of a person who is unfamiliar with the change, they will be following static, outdated advice and their resulting decision will be affected.

Furthermore, in a new and unprecedented situation, the people of influence can change quickly. One weekly coordination meeting may be attended on a single occasion by a senior government member, who stipulates that certain conditions must be fulfilled in order for organisations to continue operating. Yet their instructions may soon be forgotten as time goes by without their presence. An organisation may have been present at the senior government member's meeting, and now be following the advice. They will then insist that their staff follow the procedure, even if that procedure is well out of date and is no longer adhered to in daily operations. This will bring that organisation into conflict with others who aren't aware of those requirements. If a group meeting in a very changeable situation says, "as NGOs we don't do this," that approach may be appropriate for that particular week. But situations change all the time. Be willing to take on board new approaches if they are more suitable. Recognise that the moment you sat in that meeting was one small point in time, with a lot of different approaches before it, and a lot of future changes ahead of it.

Making good, effective decisions in disaster response involves recognising that situations are dynamic. Don't take a static statement at one point in time, for example at a cluster, as being the definitive position. On a different week, with different people in the room the guidance might be completely different. Avoid building policies based on the outcome of one meeting.

Cooperation

Any large-scale response, particularly one involving work in fixed locations such as emergency shelter venues or camps, is going to involve working around other organisations. In many cases your activities and theirs will be complementary, or overlapping. But occasionally your activities will be in conflict with the approach of another organisation. In order to avoid this conflict growing and affecting your activities, aim to follow a few guiding points.

Firstly, try to recognise the interests of the other organisation. What are they trying to achieve? What outcomes are important for them? What pressures – donor, governmental, or other – may be driving them, behind the scenes? Understanding their interests and the pressures that they are under may help you identify a good solution.

Secondly, try to distinguish between life-threatening risks, and the minor hazards that are inevitable in relief situations. Is your programme addressing a minor hazard, while theirs addresses a much greater risk? In that case, you may need to adjust your approach until the major risk has first been dealt with. Conversely, you may judge that your own initiative is addressing a much greater issue. Try to weigh up the absolute necessity of your action and theirs, which will have a significant impact on the direction that your decision takes.

Thirdly, aim to assess immediate needs against predictable future needs. For example, consider the case of a transit camp for about one thousand people per day, running in a remote location. People often spend as little as 30 minutes in the camp before being bused away to a larger venue. The camp is run from a fairly small petrol generator. The camp's logistics manager wants the generator to have a resting period during the day, as it is in constant use at night providing power for safety and security lighting. He has concerns that if it is overused and damaged, the camp will be without essential power throughout the night. The telecommunications organisation which was asked to provide displaced people with a means to contact other family members needs the generator to run in order for their satellite communications equipment to function. They were told there would be power provided for their equipment to run. Turning off the generator deprives people of the ability to contact family with an update on their whereabouts. Family reunification and protection of vulnerable individuals has become a priority, but so has the safety of all those in the camp during the night. If asked to judge what should be done about the situation, what would you decide?

In the example, some adequate solutions might include: running the generator for shorter periods with frequent breaks during the day, such as a 30 minute on; 30 minute off system; advising people to stay longer in the camp if phone services are a priority to them; committing to run the generator more as long as the telecoms group provide a second generator within 48 hours; asking other organisations in the camp if they can source a generator; finding out how close the next camp with telecoms services is and advising people that they can check for their family there. These suggestions are not the only compromise solutions possible, but they provide an indication of the type of acceptable compromises which are necessary in order to find a 'good enough' solution.

Making a good decision in such a situation involves understanding the interests of each organisation. By discovering these interests, any solution which appears to cover both group's key points will naturally present itself as acceptable. In many disaster response situations, an acceptable decision is one which is adequate in the short run. A more comprehensive solution can be developed over time, but in the meantime the organisations in conflict can each continue with their main goal.

Other Organisations:

Principles to remember

CHAPTER EIGHT

DAILY CHALLENGES

Ask any experienced humanitarian worker and they will have examples of situations that were particularly challenging. Listen to enough of these examples, and you will begin to pick up patterns of common problems. These problems might include such things as: crowds getting out of control at distributions; not having the right documents to allow an activity to take place; accidents or serious illnesses affecting staff; fraudulent activities by suppliers or staff members; restrictive government policies that hinder activities; and situations changing rapidly and without warning.

Working through the some of these potential problems in advance, and having strategies for dealing with them, can allow you to make quick, assertive decisions when a similar situation occurs. It can also help you to develop clear guidelines among colleagues to ensure that your organisation responds with consistency.

Scenario Eight

As security conditions in the surrounding countryside (Scenario Six) have deteriorated, your team has increasingly needed to make use of aircraft charters. Most of your medical distributions now involve transporting goods and support staff by light aircraft.

You and your team have appreciated the difference that the air transport makes, and you have built up a good relationship with the air charter company. The company works with you to get the maximum use out of the aircraft on the days when you use it. Still, they always stress the need to be ready ahead of time, so that the day's activities can keep moving as planned. You have learned from experience that when you hold up the flights, the last one or two stops on your flight end up getting missed, with the goods being returned to your base for distributing at a later time.

This morning you have a flight due in. It's close to a national holiday, and from tomorrow much of the country will shut down for two weeks. You are feeling the pressure to make sure the flight completes its full route, since any missed locations may have to wait a long time before being re-supplied.

You're driving the work pickup truck with a separate trailer attached behind. Both are heavily loaded with medical supplies. Your colleague is in the passenger terminal, helping process the three volunteer medical staff who will be flying out to one of the remote clinics.

From the vehicle parking area you watch your chartered aircraft materialise out of the pale blue sky. As it touches down and taxis along the runway you start the drive out to meet it at the apron where light aircraft park. Near the entrance to the apron, on a service road, you spot a large passenger bus. Covering the side of the bus is the logo of a large, international organisation. The bus has stopped, waiting for its own aircraft to shut down its engines. You drive past it, scanning for where your own charter will stop. Just as you are about to turn onto the apron you hear a loud crash. There's a crunch, a scrape of metal, and the sound of shattering glass.

Shocked, you look back in your side mirror. The bus has tried to turn after you passed, but the driver hadn't allowed for the trailer. The side of your trailer and the front corner of the bus are both crumpled from the impact.

You've been briefed on the rules of the road and what to do when accidents occur. You should keep the vehicle where it is, and let the police come to make a report. But your aircraft is now parked over half a kilometre away. Some of your cargo is bulky and heavy, especially the bales of mosquito nets. Loading the plane from here will add more than an hour to the day's schedule. You realise that the airfield is technically private land, and that the rules of the road might not apply here.

Do you move the vehicle to the aircraft?

Yes: go to 1

Maybe: go to 2

Otherwise: go to 7

1 You decide that your priority is getting the goods on board the aircraft. Also, in the weeks that you have been chartering the aircraft you have built up some good relationships at the airport. You feel sure that this should help you resolve the issue. You drive away from the crash site and over to the parked aircraft. After updating the pilot on the situation and giving her your final cargo weight, you begin to untie the restraining straps that hold your cargo in place. While you work on the straps the pilot begins calculating the final route on her tablet.

You have barely started when a jeep pulls up with some very agitated men inside. The jeep bears the same logo as the passenger bus. The men jump out and accuse you of fleeing a crash site. They insist that you have to return immediately and wait for the police. Their organisation has strong links with the government, and many NGOS look to it for access and protection in disaster situations. Staying on the right side of this organisation has helped many NGOs gain better access to government support. However, you're aware from a recent course you took that the organisation has no direct authority over NGOs working in the country.
Do you follow their instructions to move back?

Yes: Go to 4   Otherwise go to 6

2 You think that it may be better if you inform the bus driver before you simply drive away from the site of a crash. Still, with the time pressure you don't want to get into a long argument about who was at fault.

Do you talk to the bus driver?

Yes: go to 3   Otherwise go to 7

3 You think that the process may go more smoothly if you speak with the bus driver before deciding whether to move.

The driver is still in his seat, inside the bus. You walk over to his side window. He winds the window down and you explain that you have cargo to load and that you can't stay where you are. You explain that you will remain on the airfield afterwards and discuss what to do about the accident.

The bus driver simply shrugs at you. He looks very nervous and you realise he is more concerned about what his bosses will say about the crash than anything else.

Go to 1

4 You explain to the pilot that you simply have to move back to the site of the crash. She shows you the timetable she has calculated. She explains that any delay is going to mean missing the last planned stop of the day, and any more than an hour's delay will mean missing the stop before that as well.

One of the men from the jeep interrupts and says you need to move back immediately. Ignoring him, the pilot tells you that you have no choice but to load, if you want to complete the planned route.

Do you still follow the jeep back to the crash site?

Yes: Go to 5   Otherwise go to 6

5 You decide the only way to proceed is to have the vehicle at the crash site until it can be cleared by the authorities. You tell the people around you that you are available once a police officer comes to take a report. You call your colleague and ask him to see if he can arrange another truck from one of the other aircraft companies. Ten minutes later he comes over with a flatbed trailer. "It's all I could find," he says.

Normally the trailer would be pulled in a line with several others by an airport tractor. But you realise you will have to pull it by hand. Enlisting the help of your colleague, the pilot, and the three volunteer medical staff, you begin the process of transferring the cargo to the plane. Within minutes you're all sweating heavily. The cargo requires four trips with the trailer. Each time you return to the vehicle you check for the authorities, but none have arrived.

When the final cargo is loaded, you return to the pickup truck and watch the aircraft take off. Several boxes of medical supplies remain on the truck. The pilot had explained that due to the time taken loading, the last two destinations would have to be dropped. You tried to persuade her otherwise, pointing out the two-week break before normal activities can continue. Yet the best she could offer was to drop some other locations from the routing instead. It was clear that whatever option you took, some clinics were going to go un-stocked.

As you deal with the disappointment of knowing some locations won't get their supplies, you look up and see two policemen walking towards you. You sigh, knowing you have a long day ahead of you before you get anything resolved.
Go to 11

6 You tell the men in the jeep that your priority is your cargo, and the needs of the people in the clinics you are supplying. They are furious, and tell you that they are going to bring the airport director. You concentrate on loading the cargo.

You are almost finished loading when they return, bringing with them a stern, elderly man who you recognise as the airport director. He climbs out of the jeep and the men surround him.

"Was that your crash site?" he asks. You reply that it was. The men ask him to make you go back. Immediately he turns on them.

"I've seen your bus drivers. They go far too fast and are a danger to everyone. I have no doubt it was their fault."

The men are stunned, and you're quietly delighted. But then his next reply surprises you.

"I don't have time to sort out driving disputes. You need to go and see the police outside the airport gate. They'll deal with the incident. Now, drive me back to my office." He climbs back into the jeep. Two of the men climb in with him, and they drive off.

The pilot calls you over. "I can handle the loading from here," she says. "Why don't you go and do what you need to do with the police? As long as you don't mind walking. Just leave the truck here and I'll finish off."

You motion to the two remaining men from the other organisation. You notice that they have cooled down a bit from their earlier anger, and you explain that you need to fetch the police.

"I'm not sure we should do that," one says. "You know, there's this holiday coming up. They're going to impound the vehicles, and we won't see them until after the break."

You realise he's right. The truck is essential to your work and you can't afford to lose it for two weeks.

"Well, from our side, we can deal with this," he continues. "But we need you to sign a waiver saying it wasn't our fault. You won't have to pay anything. Just sign that you won't try to claim anything from us. Otherwise it has to go through our formal channels. We'll be forced to make a police report, have the vehicles impounded, and so on. It's just the way our system works."

You look at your trailer. The damage to it is fairly minimal.

Do you sign a waiver?

Yes: go to 8

Maybe: go to 9

Otherwise go to 10

7 You decide to remain where you are until you at least see the police. You call your colleague in the terminal and ask him to come out with the airport authorities.

You think that the process may go more smoothly if you speak with the bus driver. But the bus driver simply shrugs at you. He looks very nervous and you realise he is more concerned about what his bosses will say about the crash than anything else.

Five minutes pass, and there's no sign of your colleagues or the airport authorities. You feel sure that the air traffic controller will have seen the incident from up in the tower, but they don't appear to have notified anyone. As you wait, a jeep full of men pulls up. The men spill out of their vehicle and start to accuse you of causing the accident. They appear to be from the same organisation as the bus driver.

Just then the pilot arrives. She's seen your vehicle and has walked across to find out what the delay is. She talks with you for a minute, then shows you the timetable she has calculated. She explains that any delay is going to mean missing the last planned stop of the day, and any more than an hour's delay will mean missing the stop before that as well. She tells you that you really need to get the cargo to the plane right away, and then deal with the crash paperwork later. She also confirms that the airfield is private land and that it is under the control of the aviation authorities, not the police.

Do you move the vehicle to begin loading the aircraft?

Yes: go to 6

Otherwise go to 5

8 You decide to sign the waiver. The man asks you to follow him to their airport office. You are treated well, and the waiver form is eventually produced. As you read through the form before signing it, you realise that you have clear grounds to contest it if they ever try to charge you for repairs to the bus.

You hear the high pitch of an engine and look out of the office window. As you watch your aircraft take off, you glance at your watch. You notice that the take-off is well within the timeframe that the pilot had given. You relax, as you realise that you have done as much as you can in making sure the full routing gets completed. You know how grateful the different clinics and their patients will be.

Go to 11

9 You are mindful that the group could use a waiver to try to charge you, despite what they say about that not being the reason for it. However, you realise that you could claim that you were under duress when you signed, due to the situation - and so the waiver would not be legally binding.

As you consider this, the man notes your hesitation. "This happens all the time. We're such a big organisation that people often try to claim from us. That's why we have the waiver, to stop that happening."

Do you sign the waiver?

Yes: go to 8

Otherwise go to 10

10

You decide that you don't want to sign a waiver. For all you know, the organisation could then use it to try to claim for repairs to their bus.

The man is clearly disappointed. "Looks like our afternoon is gone then. We're going to be filling in forms at that police station for a long time. At least let's stop by the sandwich bar on our way there. I don't know what time we'll be finished."

The pilot confirms that she is well ahead of schedule now. As soon as the passengers arrive, she tells you, they'll be going. You relax a little, as you realise that you have done as much as you can in making sure the full routing gets completed. You know how grateful the different clinics and their patients will be.

Thirty minutes later you are not so relaxed. You are at the police station, and have just been told that your truck will be impounded until they can follow up on the paperwork. With the coming holiday, that won't be for at least another two weeks. You have plans to continue local distributions during the holidays, and realise you will have to hire a local truck. With all the NGOs in town, and the way the prices have risen, that's going to cost you hundreds of dollars. You wonder how much repairs to the bus might have cost.

Go to 11

11

The two-week holiday has passed, and things are back to normal. In the government notices which often follow the end of the holiday, a change to the NGO Act was announced. Now all heads of agency will have to complete a form every six months which lists international employees and their qualifications.

As the most senior staff member in the team at the current time, you have the responsibility for signing. You have driven thirty minutes across the city to the recently finished government office.

You walk into the office. A clerk sits at a shiny new desk. In the corner, a sleepy-looking soldier sits, a folded newspaper on his lap. You ask if the director is available. Barely glancing up from his phone, the clerk tells you that the director is busy. He gestures to a bank of chairs under the window.

Do you wait?

Yes: go to 12

Maybe: go to 13

Otherwise go to 14

12 You sit down. Twenty minutes pass with no sign of change. In your mind you are running through the list of all you have to do. You start to worry that you will lose your whole morning.

A few minutes later a man walks in. He's clearly foreign, but seems at ease in the surroundings. He greets the clerk warmly. The clerk responds with a smile and starts asking about his work and his family. It's obvious that they have known each other for some time.

"Is the director in?" the foreigner asks eventually, pointing towards the inner office.

"Sure, go ahead," the clerk replies, to your surprise. The foreigner walks towards the director's door.

Do you try to follow him in?

Yes: go to 15   Otherwise go to 16

13 You ask the clerk how long it will be before you can see the director.

"I'm not sure. He'll be ready when he's ready."

You think of all you have to do in the day.

Do you sit and wait?

Yes: go to 12   Otherwise go to 14

14 You decide that you don't want to waste your whole morning waiting without any idea of when you will have an appointment. You ask the clerk if you can fix a time to meet the director.

His reply is blunt. "The director doesn't wait for you. You wait for him."

You run through the list of all you have to do. You also think about how essential the new paperwork is, to allow your supply of foreign staff to keep coming in to fulfil some of their specialist roles. You decide that you will just have to wait things out. **Go to 12**

15 You decide to stand up and follow the foreigner in to the director's office.

"Hey," the clerk shouts out. "You can't go in there."

The soldier gets to his feet and turns to you. "You'd better do as he says," he tells you. **Go to 18**

16 You don't want to be seen to be barging in to the office unannounced. But it seems clear that the director can manage interruptions.

Do you ask the clerk if you can also go in?

Yes: go to 17   Otherwise go to 18

17 You ask if you can go in now. By way of response, the clerk calls you over to his desk. "Before you go in, let me see your paperwork." You hand him the file of documents, and he studies it for a few minutes, pausing on the last page.

"See, your problem is here." He points to an area of white space on the paper. "You need this stamped from the Ministry of Foreign Affairs before it can be accepted here."
You look at your watch. It's close to lunch time. You realise you'll have to get the Ministry's stamp in the afternoon, then return here the following morning. You feel very frustrated as you realise that your afternoon and the following morning will be used up getting the paperwork completed.

You start to head out of the office. Do you take time to thank the clerk as you leave?

Yes: go to 21   Otherwise go to 22

18 You continue to wait. After ten more minutes the director's door opens, and the foreigner walks out. He nods his thanks at the clerk and walks towards the door. As he does, you catch his eye. He smiles and stops for a moment.

"Didn't I see you at that medical coordination meeting a few weeks ago? I'm good at remembering faces but not names, I'm afraid." You introduce yourself briefly, wondering if he could help you with getting to see the director.

Do you ask for his assistance?

Yes: go to 19   Otherwise go to 20

19 You decide to ask the foreigner for his help.

"Sure, I can have a look for you. Let's see your paperwork." You give him your file of documents. He takes it over to the clerk's desk, chats with the clerk for a few moments then spreads the papers out on the clerk's desk. Together the foreigner and the clerk flick through the various sheets.

After a moment the foreigner calls you over.

"See, your problem is here." He points to an area of white space on the paper. "You need this stamped from the Ministry of Foreign Affairs before it can be accepted here."

You look at your watch. It's close to lunch time. You realise that you will have to get the ministry's stamp in the afternoon, then return to this office the following morning. You feel very frustrated as you realise that your afternoon and the following morning will be used up getting the paperwork completed.

You start to head out of the office. Do you take time to thank the clerk as you leave?

Yes: go to 21

Otherwise go to 22

20

You decide to keep waiting. Occasionally, you ask the clerk if the director has become available, but the answer is always to wait.

After about 40 minutes the clerk calls you over.

"Before you go in, let me see your paperwork." You hand him the file of documents, and he studies it for a few minutes, pausing on the last page.

"See, your problem is here." He points to an area of white space on the paper. "You need this stamped from the Ministry of Foreign Affairs before it can be accepted here."

You look at your watch. It's close to lunch time. You realise that you will have to get the ministry's stamp in the afternoon, then return to this office the following morning. You feel very frustrated as you realise that your afternoon and the following morning will be used up getting the paperwork completed.

You start to head out of the office.

Do you take time to thank the clerk as you leave?

Yes: go to 21

Otherwise go to 22

21

Despite your feelings of frustration, you take a moment to stop and thank the clerk for his help.

He looks at you, slightly surprised. After a moment's pause he replies.

"That's okay. I'm sorry that you've been delayed. I'm sure when you come back tomorrow you'll be able to get everything finished."

As you leave the office, some of your frustration dissolves. You feel like having the clerk on your side will make your next visit go a lot more smoothly. **Go to 23**

22

You're finding it hard to hide your feelings of frustration. You stride out of the office, thinking about all the extra steps you have to take in order to get a simple task done.

The foreigner walks out of the office behind you.

"If I can give you a word of advice?" he asks. "You know, no matter how much these processes frustrate you, you need to keep it hidden. You have to stay polite, stay patient. The moment you let someone see they're getting to you, they might well delay things even more. If you can, try to get clerks like that guy on your side. You don't have to like them. But it just makes the work go so much smoother."

You think about his advice. You realise that it is easier said than done. **Go to 23**

23 Late that afternoon you're back in your office. Your logistician, Patrick, enters the office with an odd look on his face. You often use him for tasks that require good local networks, since he was born in the area and has lots of strong connections in the community. Patrick tells you that while he was parked downtown, his briefcase was stolen from his car. You know that the briefcase had $300 in it earmarked to pay the owner of a hotel that you often use for short-term visitors.

You know that Patrick is naturally very cunning. He recently solved some very challenging issues with some customs paperwork relating to your medical supplies, saving you a lot of time and money. However, you also know that he has a lot of personal debt.

Do you ask for a police report of the theft?

Yes: go to 24

Otherwise go to 25

24 You ask him for the police report of the theft.

"I tried to file a report," he says. "I called a policeman to come and look but he said there is nothing they can do for something like this. He said that it was my fault for leaving the door unlocked."

Go to 25

244

25

You have your suspicions about the whole incident. It seems quite convenient given Patrick's debts.

You think about how to deal with the lost $300.

Do you tell him you are charging the loss to his personal staff account?

Yes: go to 26

Maybe: go to 27

Otherwise go to 29

26

You tell Patrick that it was his negligence that was the cause of the loss, and that you will be charging him because of it.

He looks crestfallen. "I can't afford this. There's no way I can pay it. I'll have to take a job in the mines if I want to pay it off."

You realise that once he leaves the organisation there is no way that you will ever recover the money. You will also face a big challenge finding such an effective logistician to fill his place. He knows the local systems and has whole webs of local connections.

Do you look for an alternative solution to charging him?

Yes: go to 29

Otherwise go to 28

27

You tell Patrick that it was his negligence that was the cause of the loss, and that you will be charging him part of the cost because of it. You tell him that the organisation will cover half the loss but that he has to bear some responsibility.

He looks crestfallen. "I can't afford this. There's no way I can pay it. I'll have to take a job in the mines if I want to pay it off."

You realise that once he leaves the organisation there is no way that you will ever recover the money. You will also face a big challenge finding such an effective logistician to fill his place. He knows the local systems and has whole webs of local connections.

Do you look for an alternative solution to charging him?

Yes: go to 29

Otherwise go to 28

28 You decide that you have no choice but to impose the financial penalty. When you tell him what you are going to do, Patrick tells you he will have to quit immediately.

You think about holding back Patrick's remaining salary, to cover some of the loss. But then you remember your last challenge at the labour court. You decide it's easier just to let him go.

In the weeks that follow, you face several small issues at the customs department, due to problems with the paperwork on your medical shipments. The new logistician that you have hired is out of his depth and is unable to find good solutions. One evening as you are checking the accounts and you realise that all the small fines to resolve these problems have added up to over $700. You wonder how much it would have been if Patrick had still been with you. **Ends.**

29 While you are considering your other options, the team driver comes into the office. You both greet him, with Patrick breaking into the usual longer greeting in the language that they both share. After hanging up the vehicle keys, the driver steps outside to go to the water fountain. Your phone rings, and while you answer it, Patrick steps outside to talk to the driver.

On one side of your office is a window that looks out over the eating area.

Do you walk across to watch the encounter between Patrick and the driver?

Yes: go to 30   Otherwise go to 31

30

Continuing your phone call, you walk across to the window, where you can look down on the eating area.

You watch Patrick in discussion with the driver. You're not an expert in body language, but you can tell from the driver's folded arms, and tilted head, that he seems quite skeptical of what he is being told.

You have a strong suspicion that Patrick's actions involve fraud, but you have no real way to determine it for certain.

You have to decide what to do with Patrick.

Do you offer a formal reprimand?

Yes: go to 32

Otherwise go to 33

31

You decide that you don't want to be seen 'spying' on your staff. You turn your full attention to the phone call until it is finished.

You have a strong suspicion that that Patrick's actions involve fraud, but you have no real way to determine it for certain.

You have to decide what to do with Patrick.

Do you offer a formal reprimand?

Yes: go to 32

Otherwise go to 33

32 You call Patrick back into the office and give him a formal warning on the issue. You make it clear that if such negligence occurs again then he will have to bear the full cost of any loss.

After he leaves you find yourself wondering if you could have handled things any differently.

In the weeks that follow, you face several small issues at the customs department, due to problems with the paperwork on your medical shipments. Patrick is heavily involved in resolving the problems. One evening as you are checking the accounts, you realise that despite the potential for large charges, the small fines to resolve these problems have added up to less than $100. You wonder how much it would have cost you if you didn't have Patrick's help. Thinking about this helps you feel better about how you handled the money which was supposedly stolen. **Ends.**

33 You decide that you will just treat the theft as part of the cost of working in a tense environment.

In the weeks that follow, you face several small issues at the customs department, due to problems with the paperwork on your medical shipments. Patrick is heavily involved in resolving the problems. One evening as you are checking the accounts, you realise that despite the potential for large charges, the small fines to resolve these problems have added up to less than $100. You wonder how much it would have cost you if you didn't have Patrick's help.

Thinking about this helps you feel better about how your decision not to penalise Patrick. **Ends.**

Daily challenges

In humanitarian response, as with any type of work, certain problems occur quite frequently. Part of learning to respond well in disaster response is developing an understanding of these types of problems, anticipating them and pre-emptively planning how to respond should they develop.

For example, if you find yourself in an environment where militia forces are at work, you can predict that you will have regular problems with uneducated, ill-disciplined young militia members. You might face constant demands for payment at checkpoints, or your staff might be intimidated on a frequent basis. You might expect a disruptive presence at any distributions you conduct, and you could find that a general attitude of hostility prevails.

By recognising this as your operating environment, you can proactively plan for your encounters with militia members. Take time as a staff to discuss the challenges that you are likely to face, and agree on your preferred responses to these challenges. This doesn't mean that it will always be possible to act in a particular, pre-agreed way, but at least you will have some guiding principles to follow.

While planning as a staff, pay careful attention to your team members' personalities, and their preferred way of resolving difficult situations. Use the Corruption Response Scale as a rough, working guideline to anticipate any problems which may arise from having team members with very different viewpoints.

Insecurity and armed forces are not the only daily challenges. If traffic conditions are terrible and crashes are a regular occurrence, prepare by briefing people well on how to respond in an accident. Run role play scenarios so that team members know what to do in an incident, who to call, and which relevant documents are in the vehicle.

If government red tape causes regular delays to your project, aim to brief staff on how to respond in situations where delays occur. Help them to understand a chain of command that takes the pressure off them and allows them to refer problems to an experienced staff member.

Rather than view these and other daily challenges as problems to avoid, you can treat them as an inevitable part of your operations. By accepting their presence, you can justify giving time to planning and preparing for how to respond. As you become better prepared, certain choices will naturally present themselves as good decisions.

The daily challenges will vary by location. Once you begin to acknowledge the common problems in your particular area of operation, you will begin to see patterns of problems occurring. Using these patterns to guide you is another key step in making rapid decisions.

Situational perception

By now you will be familiar with the concept that expertise includes issues of perception. An expert sees a situation, recognises certain aspects of it, and this in turn suggests a pattern. By following the pattern through, an expert's decisions almost appear to make themselves; the expert naturally responds in the way needed to bring about the desired outcome.

In contrast, a novice can be thought of as someone who doesn't have the same familiarity with those patterns. They don't recognise them, and so they won't know what steps those patterns suggest in order to reach a favourable outcome.

Building expertise in decision making is not just a matter of practicing the individual steps in resolving a problem. Rather it involves learning to put the decision-making point into a larger context, that of an established pattern.

In the diagrams below, the dotted sphere represents the larger context in which a specific situation occurs. The specific situation itself, such as a demand for payment and the immediate tension that surrounds it, is called the 'flash point.' The flash point is any occurrence where an individual is forced to make a decision about a situation. It is represented by the star.

Figure 8.1 shows the novice's perception of the incident. The flash point, being so dominant, takes up the whole of the novice's understanding and their response.

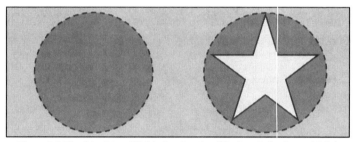

Figure 8.1. The 'big picture' (left); the situation fills the whole picture (right)

However, as a level of experience is accumulated, the individual begins to see the situation as a considerably smaller part of the context in which it is seated (figure 8.2). There is a much greater understanding of the factors that have led to the situation and far more experience of the various outcomes which could occur (represented by the light arrows.) In relation to the size to the overall context, the flash point becomes smaller.

For example, in the case of a demand for payment, the more experienced decision maker does not get so focused on the demand itself. They begin to see some of the background to the situation, such as bored individuals, people trying their luck, or people with genuine pressure on them - whether from climate, personal circumstances, or political pressure. This background understanding in turn suggests some possible actions that will lead to a good outcome. This might involve sharing food, drinks, taking time for conversation, referring to friends in positions of influence, or looking for other non-financial ways to resolve the situation. The more experienced person's understanding and experience allows them to shrink the size of the immediate problem, and they are able to see around it.

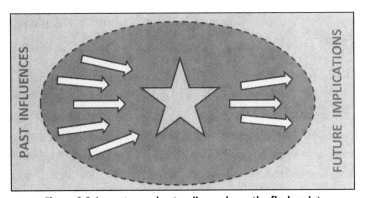

Figure 8.2 A greater understanding reduces the flash point

Eventually, at a level of considerable expertise, the whole experience merges into an indivisible flow (figure 8.3). The flash point of the situation is still present. Yet it is entirely contained within a greater understanding, one which takes the expert from a point before the occurrence of the flash point to an outcome after it has finished. The flash point itself is not distinguished from the various factors that influence its development. In turn, the eventual outcome is broader than just getting beyond the flash point.

It is because of this level of perception that an expert is able to look at a situation in advance, and use mental imagery to predict the way in which it is likely to develop.

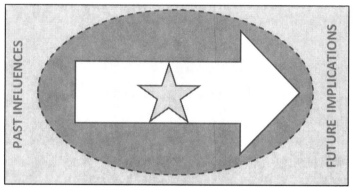

Figure 8.3 The big picture as seen by the expert

If an unexpected development occurs, the expert immediately pursues a new direction, being as familiar and confident with the new outcome as they had been with their initial forecast. In this way, a change at the flash point (figure 8.4) does not leave the expert immobilised. They do not have to struggle to generate multiple, alternative solutions. Instead, they recognise the new direction as providing a single new alternative, and follow it.

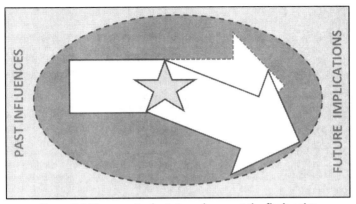

Figure 8.4 The expert adapts to a change at the flash point

Seeing patterns in disaster response

As Dr Gary Klein points out, proficient decision makers have developed the ability to detect *patterns* and *typicality*. This ability allows them to "size up a situation in a glance and realise that they have seen it, or variants of it, dozens or hundreds of times before." [1] Research by Barbara Means and her colleagues suggests that the differences between experts and novices lies more "in pattern recognition and the ability to build a rich mental representation... than in the decision processes that [are] imposed." [2] The lesson here as you seek to improve your ability to make good decisions in high pressure, humanitarian settings is to is to develop the same understanding that an expert brings to a situation. A key part of this is to focus on building up your ability to recognise patterns.

There is much to be said for real, practical experience, developed in high-pressure situations. Yet developing experience does not need to be limited to real-life events. The wide popularity of aircraft simulators and other training scenarios highlight the value of simulated training. As you have worked through the situations simulated in this book, you have not only built your understanding of the factors that help your decision-making ability, but you will also have begun to develop some recognition of typical patterns.

You can continue to develop your expertise in pattern recognition in a number of ways:

- Look for training courses which include simulated scenarios as part of their content. A number of humanitarian organisations run this type of training for their own staff, while others make their courses available to the general public. From time to time, global humanitarian clusters run large simulations which bring in people from many different organisations. Your organisation may be in a place to help you join one of these. In-person training is valuable, but an increasing amount of training is available online. Any humanitarian course which puts you in the driving seat of decision making in a humanitarian setting has value when it comes to building patterns of recognition.

- Attend talks given by humanitarian workers who have recently been in disaster situations. You may learn directly from their formal presentations; otherwise take time at the end to ask them why they took a particular approach to a specific situation. The most effective time to do this is when a person has only recently returned from their assignment – the thoughts and feelings associated with challenging points in their work will still be fresh and more easily recalled.

- If you work with colleagues who have significant frontline humanitarian experience, ask them about situations where they were under pressure to make a decision. Present them hypothetical situations, and ask them how they would respond. If you are attending a college or university course on a humanitarian subject, seek out tutors or professors with experience in high-pressure situations. Ask them what principles guided them when they undertook different relief projects.

- Look for opportunities to volunteer in a role which forces you to make decisions under pressure. This might be through involvement with a local Civil Defence or Red Cross / Red Crescent team. Any time a situation occurs where the needs outweigh the resources, decision-making pressures occur. Responding to a small-scale natural disaster in your home country can give you a sense of the same pressures that will be present in a large emergency.

- If you have a friend or acquaintance working internationally in disaster response, consider using your annual leave to visit them. Even if they are not able to offer you volunteer work, just spending time with them and their colleagues will give you a greater sense of the challenges that exist. In some situations, just getting to their area of work will force you to work your way through challenging decision points. If you decide to follow this route, make sure to get good guidance on personal safety and security well ahead of time, and stay well-informed about any changes to the overall situation. Do not put yourself at unnecessary risk just to gain experience.

- Certain films, books, and TV shows feature high-pressure decision points. Medical series are a good example. When watching or reading, pause at the point where a difficult decision presents itself. Think about a possible response to the situation. As far as possible, try to follow the single-option approach that you've been practising throughout the book.

- For those with a responsibility to train others, the chapter on 'training suggestions' will provide ideas of ways to simulate the decision environment, which will permit your students to develop greater decision-making abilities in disaster response.

Through these and other methods, aim to build up your experience in dealing with challenging decisions. As you become more familiar with the patterns involved, you will find yourself becoming more comfortable making the decisions themselves.

Daily Challenges:

Principles to remember

CHAPTER NINE

FINAL GUIDANCE

A **final word of warning:** this book refers to situations where the best way to make a quick decision is to go for a 'good enough' solution.

As previously mentioned, one feature of disaster situations is that much information is often missing. When you operate in these environments, you will find that your background knowledge may be incomplete. Current information is often limited. Goals and objectives change rapidly as new information comes to light. You operate with limited physical and financial resources, and with fewer staff than you need to do a thorough job. Other individuals and organisations with conflicting goals are a constant presence.

Normal financial and record-keeping systems may be damaged or non-existent. Within this complex, dynamic environment you are trying to operate in a manner which moves you towards your current, temporary goals.

The result is that anyone looking back at a disaster response activity is likely to have a much clearer understanding of the issues than you had at the time. More information about the situation and the needs, as well as the activities of others will have come to light. Better mapping may exist, adding to the overall clarity. These improvements can lead to people judging your actions, and the decisions you made. It's very easy for them to assume that at the point of making a decision, you had as much clear information as they now possess.

In order to become comfortable with making 'good enough' decisions, decisions which achieve your overall stated goal despite any compromises that you're forced to make, you need to become comfortable with people second-guessing those decisions. You need to carry the courage of your conviction that at the time, given your limited information, the decision you made was appropriate.

This doesn't mean ignoring good advice or suggestions. In fact, you can build your decision-making skills and judgement even further by inviting people to give feedback on your actions. But try to ensure that those commenting on your actions are people with an understanding of the complexities of the situation that you faced. Talk to experienced colleagues who won't spend time judging your actions, who will instead provide helpful guidance on ways to improve. Be willing to learn from their feedback, knowing that it will make you more effective in the next situation you face. However, avoid taking on board every piece of criticism of your actions, especially when the source of that criticism is a person who has never faced the challenges that you have been through. Anticipate this type of criticism, and prepare yourself to deal with any self-doubts that may arise from it.

Ultimately, you were the one who was willing to enter that dynamic, uncertain, fast-changing, high-stakes situation, to make the choices and take the actions that you felt were going to bring support to people in great need. If you remain open to learning – from the very people you are supporting, from experienced colleagues, from relevant post-disaster reports - then you are well on your way to making wise and effective decisions as you respond to disasters.

PART TWO :

THEORY

MAKING THE CASE FOR NATURALISTIC DECISION MAKING IN HUMANITARIAN DISASTER RESPONSE

Decision-making theory has evolved in the past fifty years. Much of the background research has been done in the field of psychology,[1] and subsequently adapted over the years by everyone from management authors and economists to the military and lifestyle coaches. The type of decision which has most strongly entered mainstream thinking is that which psychologists term "classical decision theory."[2]

Classical decision making

Classical decision making is a logical system, which "can be seen as a menu. Different possibilities… are laid out before your eyes." [3] Classical decision theory maintains that "people find it very difficult to take a lot of factors into account when making a single decision," [4] and suggests that the only solution "is to be systematic." [5]

Following the classical method implies that a decision maker will consider a series of alternative solutions to a problem. The strengths and limitations of each will be evaluated against all the others, leading to a preferred choice. Decisions, in this way of thinking, make themselves; the competent decision maker has but to identify the best outcome available amongst all options.

On one contemporary business skills website, a decision-making test tells participants who get a medium score to "concentrate on finding lots of options." [6] Participants who achieve a high score are congratulated on their ability to "generate lots of potential solutions." [7] They apparently also possess the ability to "analyze the options carefully, and make the best decisions possible based on what [they] know." [8] The website cautions that "if you simply adopt the first solution you encounter, then you're probably missing a great many even better alternatives." [9] Such a decision making approach is very valid in certain circumstances. In the example of a family deciding to buy a house, it could indeed be short-sighted to buy the first house that is available. An arguably more sensible approach would be to investigate a number of potential properties, and then compare the options based on a number of criteria, such as cost, condition of the house and the distance to other places of importance in the family's life.

Any final decision will usually be an informed compromise between various conflicting requirements.

An underlying assumption that has crept in due to the proliferation of the classical decision model is that such reasoning represents how people *think*. The model is applied not only to the way that people make somewhat abstract choices 'on paper' (such as the aforementioned list of house qualities), but also to the way the human mind works. The underlying implication is that a sufficiently aware individual will be able to mentally identify the best outcome amongst a competing set of options. An expert decision maker, then, is portrayed as someone who can work their way through a number of different options, following a mental 'decision tree,' to arrive at the best answer.

Challenging the classical model

In the 1980s and 1990s, however, a number of decision researchers started to question this approach. In reference decision trees, Zeleny notes that "although such a logical and temporal structuralization of decision making is quite useful and instructive for dealing with simple problems, it is not adequate for dealing with complexity." [10]

Whereas classical decision-making research "focuses on the decision event," [11] which can be considered to involve making a "choice from among a fixed set of known alternatives based on stable goals, purposes, and values," [12] not all decision making fits this mold. According to Zeleny,

> Decision making is a dynamic process: a complex search for information, full of detours, enriched by feedback from casting about in all directions, gathering and discarding information, fueled by fluctuating uncertainty,

indistinct and conflicting concepts – some sharp, some hazy.[13]

This complexity has been borne out in tests, for the actions observed in complex natural environments can be significantly different than "those observed in the laboratory based on decontextualized tasks performed by novices with little stake in the outcomes." [14]

As Beach and Lipshitz observe, "it is illuminating that, even when they have been trained to use classical decision theory, managers rarely use it." [15] Research by Thunholm for the Swedish military supports this observation, warning that "the main problem with the military decision-making models is that they seldom seem to be followed in the field." [16] Beach and Lipshitz further support their observation by noting that when mangers do utilise the classical approach, they "seldom follow prescriptions that disagree with their own subjective intuitions." [17] Klein, drawing on his own findings, explains that "people were not generating and comparing option sets. People were using prior experience to rapidly categorize situations. People were relying on some kind of synthesis of their experience." [18] In addition, a research group from the University of London discovered that "people who went with their initial response on a test of visual perception did better than those who were given more time to ponder." [19] Klein and his colleagues found that, in a number of different scenarios, decision making actually involved committing to a course of action where plausible alternatives existed, even if the decision maker did not identify or compare these alternatives.[20]

As it became apparent to decision researchers that subjects in many instances were not behaving according to the ideals of the classical model in real life, a number of responses occurred. Beach and Lipshitz identified four general categories of response.[21] The first was to condemn the behaviour of test subjects, criticising their inability to follow the 'ideal' logical choice. The second was to try to reduce the gap between theory and practice, by changing the subjects' behaviour. A third response involved modifying the structure of the theory, while still retaining the underlying principles.

This category included the development of 'behavioural economics.' [22] Inherent in this approach is the assumption that the underlying theory of a single 'best' option is correct. The final response was to make the practice the starting point. This fourth category took the view that by observing and "knowing what decision makers actually are attempting to do, they perhaps can be helped to do it better." [23] Scholars who follow this fourth approach have "come to believe that it is misdirected to force every, or even most decision tasks into the rather limited mold that classical theory provides." [24]

Naturalistic Decision Making

A number of scholars hold the view that human decision making is better understood by observing experienced practitioners in real life settings. Since the late 1980s they have developed an approach known as Naturalistic Decision Making (NDM). Prominent amongst these scholars is Klein, who explains that "instead of beginning with formal models of decision making, we began by conducting field research to try to discover the strategies people used." [25]

NDM challenges the claim of the classical approach that a person should develop a number of solutions with the aim of choosing the most appropriate one. Rather, it observes that experienced decision makers frequently select a solution in their mind and move forward with it, without first generating other alternatives. This approach picks up the work of Herbert Simon in the 1950s, who popularised the concept of 'satisficing' – choosing the first acceptable solution that meets the given need.[26] Simon's observations of managerial decision makers showed that they spent "a considerable amount of time identifying problems and opportunities, and assessing the situation."[27] Tellingly, he found that they spent "*most* of their time in... the *design* of suitable actions or plans. They spend the *least* amount of time in comparison and selection of options, or choice."[28] Simon introduced the concept of 'bounded rationality,' which sees attention "as the scarce resource in human decision making."[29] Since "information processing is exhausting, and potentially futile,"[30] the human action of not exploring all possible options due to limited attention appears perfectly reasonable.

Orasanu and Connolly have been extremely influential in NDM's development, identifying a number of factors which "characterize decision making in naturalistic settings."[31] These factors are: "ill-structured problems; uncertain dynamic environments; shifting, ill-defined, or competing goals; action / feedback loops; time stress; high stakes; multiple players; and organizational goals and norms."[32]

These factors create situations quite different to the far more controlled environments within which much decision making has been modelled. In behavioural economics, for example, researchers acknowledge that "life is complex, with multiple forces simultaneously exerting their influence on us."[33] Behavioural economists, recognising this complexity, aim to isolate those forces individually in order to examine each one's effect. However, in the act of doing so they create an artificial environment in which the decisions made may not accurately represent the decisions made in real life. Orasanu and Connolly cite research which found that judges and parole officers gave out sentences of different severity in the court room compared with their actions in laboratory simulations.[34] Unlike behavioural economists, NDM researchers accept that it is the interplay of many different forces which often create unique conditions, and therefore conduct their research within these complex situations. Klein can claim with some justification that "a major contribution of the naturalistic decision making community has been to describe how people actually make decisions in real-world settings." [35] Furthermore, "the NDM focus on field settings and its interest in complex conditions provide insights... about ways to improve performance." [36]

NDM provides a useful way of considering the decision-making process, for a number of reasons. Firstly, the complexity of real life means that the goals of decisions cannot always be known, for as Orasanu and Connely have observed, they can frequently alter. In such a dynamic situation, "the final decision unfolds through a process of learning, understanding, information processing, assessing, and defining the problems and circumstances." [37]

Furthermore, real life situations often contain an element of time pressure. It is the absence of any reference to such time pressure in many books on decision making which limits their value for time-pressured situations. For example, in *Ethical Decision-making and the Missionary Role*, Ramseyer writes with the underlying assumption that the cross-cultural worker has ample time on their side when making a decision.[38] Ramseyer's guidance is not transferable to the disaster relief worker faced with a time-pressured decision, such as whether or not to make an undocumented payment in order to allow emergency supplies to clear a port.

In addition, many problems faced in real life are ill-defined and ill-structured, and as a result, people often have to make decisions in the absence of a full amount of information. Klein suggests that "because most naturalistic decision problems are ill-structured, decision makers chose an option that is good enough, though not necessarily the best."[39]

Recognition-Primed Decision Making

NDM comprises a number of distinct methodologies and models, including Situation Assessment, Explanation-based Decisions, Dominance Search, Image Theory and Cognitive Control.[40] One model that has particular relevance for humanitarian disaster response is Klein's Recognition-Primed Decision Making (RPD) model. Klein explains that

> the RDP model describes how people use their experience in the form of a repertoire of patterns. The patterns highlight the most relevant cues, provide expectancies, identify plausible goals, and suggest typical types of reactions in that type of situation.[41]

The RPD model describes how experienced decision makers are able to match actual situations with these patterns. Finding a match permits a rapid decision, without the need to generate multiple possible options. A second aspect of the RPD approach involves mental simulation, "to imagine how [the decision] would play out within the context of the current situation." [42] Klein's summary is that "the RPD model is a blend of intuition and analysis." [43]

Orasanu and Connolly see three main ways in which RPD differs from the classical model:

Much effort is devoted to situation assessment or figuring out the nature of the problem; single options are evaluated sequentially through mental simulation of the outcomes; and options are accepted if they are satisfactory (rather than optimal).[44]

One evolution of RPD from the initial NDM scenarios is that it places great emphasis on the expertise of decision makers. In general, the more accomplished the decision maker, the wider their range of experience. This breadth of experience allows them to recognise the various contributing factors around a scenario which lead to an eventual decision point. As a result of Klein's emphasis on 'big-picture' expertise, the decision making process "was expanded to include a prior stage of perception and recognition of situations, as well as generation of appropriate responses."[45] One of the main contributions of RPD to the NDM field is to highlight the role of experience, whereas Orasanu and Connolly's initial factors (time-pressure, uncertain and changing goals, et cetera), did not include experience as a primary factor.[46]

RPD suggests that decisions are based, to some degree, on an individual's intuition. Flora notes that intuitions "compel us to act in specific ways, and those who lack intuition are essentially cognitively paralyzed."[47] Her analysis shows that people with the inability to generate intuition are left to decide purely via deliberate reasoning. Due to the time pressure common in many decision making situations, deliberate reasoning may not be possible. Rather, decision makers have to rely to some degree on the intuitive process. Cotter and Greif note that "many people are uncomfortable depending on intuition as a main focus of ethical decision making."[48] Nonetheless, they concede that participants in their example appeared to "rely heavily on their intuitions, built over years of observations and experience." [49] Sample concurs, having observed that in real life, decision makers "must make judgments, which are sometimes based as much on gut feeling as on precise analytical reasoning." [50]

Scott and Bruce have observed that these "intuitive and spontaneous decision making [processes] involve quick procedures and reliance on hunches." [51] Orasanu and Connolly, however, take the view that such hunches are actually the result of a person's experience, which enables them to match patterns in the current situation with similar ones experienced in the past. In this way, NDM acknowledges that decisions "are embedded in larger dynamic tasks, made by knowledgeable and experienced decision makers." [52] Following this reasoning, Orasanu and Connolly observe that expert decision makers "are distinguished from novices mainly by their situation assessment abilities, not their general reasoning skills." [53] Klein summarises this emphasis on experience: "The NDM movement shifted our conception to a knowledge-based approach exemplified by decision makers who had substantial experience." [54]

Limitations

NDM is not without its critics. Cohen and Lipshitz, both renowned authors in the field of NDM, suggest that NDM research, whilst rejecting the classical approach to decision making, "has not provided a comprehensive theory to take its place." [55] This statement appears to be based on the fact that NDM tends, on the surface, to describe rather than direct the decision making process. It does, however, ignore the significant influence which the understanding created by the

NDM approach has had on training programmes for situations where all of the ambiguities mentioned by Orasanu and Connolly exist.[56] Extensive work by Klein and colleagues in the development and facilitation of NDM-informed training gives rise to Klein's assertion that "the NDM approach has been used to improve performance through... training that is focused on decision requirements." [57] Cohen and Lipshitz propose what they see as a more holistic approach, in which they regard decisions as "graded commitments of mental, affective, or material resources to courses of action. Decision making includes a cognitive process that can create or modify such commitments." [58] This emphasis on commitment as a core of decision making is still in its infancy, and other works in press do not yet lend the theory support.

In presenting the RPD model, Klein highlights a number of situations in which it may not be appropriate. He notes that classical decision making seems to prevail when "there is a strong requirement to justify the course of action chosen." [59] Of importance to the humanitarian aid worker is that their actions will not just reflect on them, but also on their organisation. An aid worker will often feel the need to justify their decision to their colleagues, and may be required to account for that decision with their managers. It could therefore be suggested that this rules out the possibility of making single-option decisions, since, with extensive analysis, a better solution might be developed. Failing to reach this better solution may be cause for reprimand of the individual by their organisation. Since many of those working for humanitarian organisations in situations of disaster relief will be held to some level of accountability for their actions by their organisation, is it therefore reasonable to discount the value of the RPD approach?

Such reasoning is short-sighted. The author attended a contemporary emergency management training course, aimed mainly at police and fire incident commanders. The course focused on the decisions which such commanders would have to make, yet the main emphasis was on making a defensible decision.[60] Of primary importance was that the decision could later stand up under departmental review.

Scant attention was paid to the quality of the decision with regards to its suitability and impact; rather, the need to record each step taken and the ability to defend the decision took precedence. The decision makers were effectively immobilised by a fear of litigation, and by a health and safety culture which emphasizes the avoidance of risk. The challenge to humanitarian organisations involved with disaster relief is that such risk-averse approaches can permeate and render ineffective their approaches to emergency humanitarian work.

Any organisation wishing to have involvement with disaster relief must accept that such situations are inherently chaotic. Those organisations must hold their staff members to high standards of personal integrity, but never lose sight of the fact that it is the person on the ground who has been trusted to make difficult decisions under considerable pressure. Where situations of ethical ambiguity arise, that person must be free to make the best decision they possibly can, using the most appropriate means, without fear that their every act will be analysed in hindsight by committee.

Summary

In contrast to the classical decision model, it is the theories of Naturalistic Decision Making and, in particular Recognition-Primed Decision Making, which remain most suited to the conditions often found in situations of disaster relief. The increased uncertainty introduced into these situations through the presence of ethical decision points diminishes further the suitability of the classical model. It is therefore the RPD method – with its proven track record of academic validity and practical application in complex decision environments – which is proposed as the basis for a large portion of the decisions which are made in disaster response. The validity of this claim will be evaluated in the next chapter through a series of interviews with experienced humanitarian workers.

CHAPTER ELEVEN

AN INVESTIGATION OF REAL LIFE DECISION MAKERS

"If we want people to think like the experts, we have to be able to understand how the experts are thinking." [1]

The previous chapter considered the field of decision making, describing the emergence of Naturalistic Decision Making, and in particular Recognition-Primed Decision Making.

The author's belief in the appropriateness of the RPD approach for humanitarian disaster responders was reinforced by his own formal study in 2012 of the way in which people make decisions in real life disaster situations. Such an investigation would have been impossible without tangible evidence. To compile this evidence, a number of individuals involved in humanitarian work were interviewed, with the aim of gaining insight into the approaches that they employ. Of particular interest was how decisions were made where one or more of the pressures identified by Orasanu and Connolly – "ill-structured problems; uncertain dynamic environments; shifting, ill-defined, or competing goals; action / feedback loops; time stress; high stakes; multiple players; and organizational goals and norms." [2] – were present. As the aim of the study was to evaluate the effectiveness of NDM, and specifically the RPD approach, a critical hypothesis was being tested by the interviews: under the aforementioned situational pressures, did interviewees adopt a classical decision making approach, or did they act in a way more closely resembling a naturalistic approach?

The interviews took the form of semi-structured interviews. Interview subjects were asked to describe situations of pressure that they had faced. These situations were examined in depth, with decision points being extrapolated, and with the interviewees being asked to reflect on the thought processes that they employed around those decision points. The Corruption Response Scale, described in Chapter Four, was used to provide a benchmark by which to compare the standpoints of the individuals interviewed. The position of an individual on the scale is annotated as a square-bracketed number, for example [3].

Interviewees

Eight individuals were selected from a range of international humanitarian and relief organisations. The individuals all described situations where factors such as time pressure, uncertainty, changing goals, etc., played a significant part. All interviewees' responses were anonymised in order to protect the individuals and their organisations from association with specific comments.

The individuals selected each had, on average, a decade of cross-cultural experience. As such, each could be classified as an experienced decision maker in their field of work. There were two reasons for selecting experienced decision makers. Firstly, the work of Klein and others using the RPD model involves observing the actions of experienced people, so as to identify the traits of experts, not novices.[3] Secondly, the experts chosen could be asked to evaluate their current decision making process against their earlier actions as a novice. This perspective would not be available to novice decision makers.

Findings

Klein adapts the types of pressure identified by Orasanu and Connolly in his RPD research.[4] These pressures provided a useful set of categories in which to examine the responses of the interviewees, and are used as sub-headings for the following sections.

Ill-structured problems; uncertain dynamic environments; shifting, ill-defined, or competing goals

Examining a situation to put it in a bigger context was a consistent feature of subjects' responses. In reference to approaching a roadblock – a classic point for bribery or extortion to occur – one interviewee, a [2] on the Corruption Response Scale, said "I look and see what is going on *around* the situation." [5] Another individual, a [1], noted the value of "trying to be two steps ahead. Using my experience to picture what to do, and then acting accordingly." [6] Within this context, the individual could then use previous experiences to imagine how a situation would develop, in advance of it actually taking place. Although no two experiences were ever quite the same, an individual, a [5], explained that "through experience, I can prepare for a situation, ahead of it actually happening. I pre-imagine the arguments that I might have." [7] Another interviewee suggested that in this type of evolving situation "you don't really think – you react based on past experiences." [8] These statements invoke the *mental imagery* and *perception* aspects of decision making which Klein sees as foundational to the RPD approach.

Of specific relevance to disaster relief is the way the interviewees described the evolutionary nature of decision points. Such evolving decision points are commonly found in the uncertainty of disaster relief. Several individuals felt that they were better prepared for a situation if they imagined it in advance. Once the situation actually occurred, they would identify which of their imagined scenarios was unfolding, and then follow the course of action most suited to it.

Action / feedback loops

One individual, a [3], stressed that they resolved a complicated situation, not by coming up with a number of alternatives, but coming up with one solution at a time. When the first solution failed, a second solution was attempted. Each failed solution added clarity to the constraints of the problem. A suitable solution was eventually identified, although it had not been considered until previous options had failed to yield results.

Another individual, a [2], explained that they would assess how the situation was developing, to judge at which point to make a move. Experience, they explained, "leads you to know when to offer something – but it's not a bunch of choices." [9] They expanded on this by explaining that they only ever felt that they would pursue one course of action, prompted by situational cues. Any subsequent actions would be in reaction to the response they encountered, but would be singular next steps, rather than one of a choice of actions. The RPD approach makes much of experts' ability to appreciate such situational cues.

Time stress

One individual, a [4], explained that a key part of their response to time pressure was to immediately consider "the longer game, the bigger picture." [10] Another individual, a [2], noted that they would allow themselves a whole day to complete any process involving a checkpoint, regardless of their success in the past. Experience of the additional pressure brought on by time constraints caused these individuals to do everything they could to relieve those constraints as an integral part of their solutions. In both cases, however, they described responding to the situations as they presented themselves, following what they felt was the most appropriate response. Neither felt that they stopped and considered multiple options, despite using their experience to create a buffer of time. Even though allowing more time opened up the possibility of making multiple decisions, neither individual elected to use the increased time for this purpose.

High stakes

A number of individuals discussed situations where they faced the potential of severe injury and possibly death. The choices which must be made in disaster response often involve high stakes, whether in the form of risks to the lives of beneficiaries or to the aid workers themselves. A highly experienced individual, a [1], recalled that, under extreme pressure, they were "not in a position to follow a logical decision making process." [11] In that situation, they reacted to opportunities as they arose, rather than generating a number of possible options. Another individual, who claimed that they had started off their cross-cultural work as a [1], but through years of exposure to different cultures had become a [5], also reflected on a time when lives were at risk: "I don't think I considered lots of options... I don't remember ever reflecting." [12]

The findings of the preceding three sections are very revealing. They show that individuals are not operating as the classical method suggests; they are not considering multiple options. Rather, they are pursuing single options, without generating alternatives. Only when an option is found to be unsuitable do they generate a subsequent option. This approach shows great similarity to Klein's findings.

Multiple players

An individual, a [3], was relatively inexperienced in conflict situations, yet had responsibility for pulling out a number of staff at short notice from an insecure area. Such deteriorating security situations are a feature of relief in many countries. 'On the spot' decisions, which have consequences for many people, must frequently be made. The individual in question explained that they took the advice of key colleagues in order to generate a few select options. They also consulted with the local community, but, in comparison with a prolonged decision where more time was available, in this case "the consultations only lasted ten minutes." [13] They described the value of having the increased knowledge of context which came from involving other experienced staff. Despite the time pressure, they still tried to find the time to consult with others.

Various individuals spoke of being aware of the repercussions of their actions on subsequent workers. Some mentioned, for example, that they felt that taking a soft approach to bribery would make it harder for those who followed. Almost all interviewees mentioned the effect of others' actions at some point in their interviews.

Organizational goals and norms

One individual, a [3], reported that on occasion they did respond to situations with the knowledge that their actions may be reviewed by a wider group within the organisation. They suggested that on such occasions, this sense that their actions would be judged led to them being more cautious in ambiguous situations.

Another individual, also a [4], described how their head office, a [1], was commonly regarded by frontline staff as being "out of touch with the reality of the work we are doing." [14] Within their organisation, front line staff placed greater reliance on the value judgements espoused by their country-level leaders, who were felt to have a more realistic understanding of the ethical conflicts arising from the situation. They felt that their decisions needed to fall within the range of what their country leaders, rather than their international leaders, deemed appropriate.

One organisation permitted four of its individual members to act as interview subjects. This had great value as it allowed a comparison of the approaches of various individuals within the organisation, shedding light upon the assumption of the Corruption Response Scale, that an organisation would encompass a range of values. The interviewees' positions were [1], [2], [4] and [5]. The individuals at each extreme both had a significant number of years of working in cross-cultural contexts. This range of responses within a single organisation supported the hypothesis that organisations with sufficiently mature staff could encompass a range of approaches. Whilst the organisation clearly had an overall culture and norms, there appeared to be room within these norms for individuals to make decisions based on their own sense of appropriate action.

Summary

The interviews covered a range of pressured situations. There was only one instance in which an interviewee described generating multiple options, and it is possible that this was due to their level of inexperience with the specific security situation in question.

Almost exclusively, where uncertainty was present, the interview subjects reported responding in an identical manner to the process described in the RPD approach. The generation of single option responses, as well as use of mental simulation and pattern matching, were key features of the interviewees' responses.

CHAPTER TWELVE

IMPLICATIONS FOR TRAINING

The findings of the interviews appear to lend significant support for the approach suggested by Klein's Recognition-Primed Decision Making model. Of particular interest is that many of the cross-cultural experts interviewed expressed a tendency to employ a 'single option generation' approach to decision events, even when few of the pressures identified by Orasanu and Connolly were present. The evidence shows that the RPD model reflects what experts are doing in practice – it has good value as a descriptor.

The RPD approach, in combination with the Corruption Response Scale, has considerable implications for the training of humanitarian workers when it comes to developing decision-making skills In addition to interviewing front line humanitarian decision makers, the investigation was extended to consider the role of training organisations. The findings of these subsequent interviews with training providers are considered below. Four specific, yet interwoven aspects stand out.

Realism

One challenge identified by Means et al is that, when decision making skills are considered in a task context, training should "take into account the specific characteristics of the task and the social and organizational context within which it is performed."[1] They also note that "rather than being an abstract, independent task, a real-life choice will be embedded in a web of cross-cutting activities, goals, and emotions."[2]

Two of the training providers interviewed stressed the need for realism in their endeavours. A key point was raised by one humanitarian organisation, which explained that one of the main strengths of their training was the introduction, over a period of several days, of a significant amount of sleep deprivation. The trainer pointed to their organisation's desire to see people under realistic pressure, not just when they were at their best. The training provider emphasised the changes of personality which they saw in people who were put under a period of sleep-deprived stress. Their experience showed, in a manner reflected by the Corruption Response Scale, that people reacted to situations quite differently once situational stress was applied.

Training providers such as Thunholm[3] have used the RPD approach as grounds from which to argue for greater realism in their training. This seems to hold for humanitarian decision making: a more realistic programme demonstrates to trainees how people can in fact change their approach under different circumstances by allowing them to them experience the phenomenon in person. Through immersion in realistically complex training scenarios, trainees can be exposed to the "collective chaos" [4] which Mintzberg [5] sees as inherent in dynamic work environments.

This suggests a number of possibilities for introducing realistic pressure into training situations. Some of these could include:

- The introduction of a degree of sleep deprivation to recreate the mental state experienced by many humanitarian workers enduring long days in physically draining circumstances.

- The coordination of training sessions so that trainees miss expected meals in order to mimic the experience of a long, drawn out day at a visa processing office.

- Where trainees have children and the course provides childcare, running sessions beyond the time at which they were due to meet their children to inject a high level of tension into a situation.

- The construction of scenarios to ensure that trainees experience a degree of discomfort due to heat, cold or rain, to counter the lack of realism experienced in classroom discussions.

- The creation of 'unfair' situations to recreate in trainees the levels of frustration normally experienced after lengthy periods of delay.

- The payment of bribes by actors (who appear as other trainees), to encourage similar behaviour from the trainees themselves, allowing trainees to understand, in hindsight, how readily they may compromise where such compromise appears normal.

- The introduction of other sensory distractions – such as the faked injury of a trainee – to help recreate the multiple pressures that often accompany high pressure decision points.

A note of caution must be added for situations where extra realism is applied, since "determining when to introduce stress, and how much stress training is necessary, is still an art." [6]

Frequency

As Means et al note, "given that pattern recognition is important, the training issue is, 'How do we build up such patterns?'" [7] Since pattern recognition is the by-product of familiarity, there appears to be no substitute for repeated exposure to pattern-generating experiences. Training simulations are extremely valuable in this regard, for they "present problems that are designed around patterns that are common and useful in expert reasoning ... and provide many more trials than would occur naturally." [8]

Through the use of careful simulations, the key decision points found within disaster response environments can be replicated and repeated. The value of aircraft simulators is that they allow pilots to repeatedly face problems such as instrument failures that would normally only occur on an occasional basis, thus rapidly building the pilots' familiarity with the patterns associated with those failures. Similarly, a training programme could be designed to allow participants to move from one version of a high-pressure situation to another, with different actors and locations but similar underlying themes. The use of multiple instances of similar scenarios would allow trainees to rapidly reach a high level of familiarity with the patterns of such situations.

Feedback

One aspect of decision making which impacts upon training is that "many natural decision tasks do not offer clear, timely feedback." [9] Means et al suggest that one strategy for overcoming this is to "allow student decision makers to compare their solutions to those of one or more recognised experts." [10]

If this is to be undertaken, a question arises in regards to the timing of such comparisons. Should a scenario be halted by an expert as it is in progress, so that the expert can offer their suggestions? Or would this interruption unhelpfully disrupt the flow of the role play scenario? One compromise could be the use of video recordings of simulations. These recordings could be played back to trainees during debrief sessions, with experts able to interject during the process. Future scenarios could then be modified to permit trainees to encounter the specific types of circumstance which experts had identified as needing improvement.

Perspective

One of the study's disaster responder interviewees explained that prior to working cross-culturally she had been a [1]. As a result of years of cross-cultural exposure she had become a [6], but she experienced real difficulty in explaining this to people from her home country. A similar challenge exists for training providers who seek to present different approaches to a decision scenario as valid to trainees who will predominantly be [1]s. The value of the Corruption Response Scale is that it can assist trainees, not only in understanding the range of approaches which people can take, but also in beginning to conceptualise how people, under certain conditions, can adjust their own personal stance. Trainees can be helped in broadening their decision making perspective, being introduced to viewpoints such as those of Sample, who suggests that a truly effective decision maker "needs to be able to see the shades of grey inherent in a situation in order to make wise decisions." [11] They can also be helped to understand that they "cannot expect the processes that work in [their] own cultural context to have the same meanings or outcomes in another." [12]

Summary

A novice can develop an increased level of decision making expertise both by expanding their range of knowledge, and by wrestling with the implications of their value system in order to improve their perceptional ability. Suitably designed training programmes can greatly aid this process, and should be considered by all organisations involved with disaster relief.

In addition to providing students with technical subject

matter about a particular area of humanitarian response, aid organisations are encouraged to train people on practical decision-making methods. Undertaking this approach will help future frontline workers to better apply their skillsets in high-pressure, post-disaster situations. Ultimately, the quality of those decisions should lead to a greater amount of good being provided for the benefit of a greater number of recipients.

ENDNOTES

Introduction

[1] Gary Klein *Sources of Power. How People Make Decisions.* Cambridge, MA: MIT Press, 1999.

See also the more recent: Gary Klein, *Streetlights and Shadows: Searching for the Keys to Adaptive Decision Making.* Cambridge, MA: MIT Press, 2011.

Chapter Two

[1] International Federation of Red Cross and Red Crescent Societies *Principles of Conduct for the International Red Cross and Red Crescent Movement and NGOs in Disaster Response Programmes* http://www.ifrc.org/en/publications-and-reports/code-of-conduct/

To fully understand the principles of the Code see the complete version at http://www.ifrc.org/Global/Publications/disasters/code-of-conduct/code-english.pdf (accessed October 27, 2016).

[2] Bernard Adeney, *Strange Virtues: Ethics in a Multicultural World.* Downers Grove, IL: IVP, 1995, 162.
[3] Ibid., 161.

[4] Malcolm Gladwell, *Blink: The Power of Thinking without Thinking,* (London: Penguin, 2005), 114
[5] Ibid., 111.

Chapter Eight

[1] Klein, *Sources of Power*, 151.

[2] Barbara Means et al., "Training Decision Makers for the Real World," in *Decision Making in Action: Models and Methods*, eds. Gary A. Klein et al., (Norwood, NJ: Ablex, 1993), 312.

Chapter Ten

[1] Lee Roy Beach and Raanan Lipshitz, "Why Classical Decision Theory is an Inappropriate Standard for Evaluating and Aiding Most Human Decision Making," in *Decision Making in Action: Models and Methods*, eds. Gary A. Klein et al., (Norwood, NJ: Ablex, 1993), 21.
[2] Ibid.

[3] Alison Hardingham, *How to make successful decisions.* London: Sheldon Press, 1988, 4.
[4] Ibid., 62.
[5] Ibid.

[6] MindTools.com "How good is your decision-making?" http://www.mindtools.com/pages/article/newTED_79.htm (accessed October 30, 2016).
[7] Ibid.
[8] Ibid.
[9] Ibid.

[10] Milan Zeleny, *Multiple Criteria Decision Making*, (New York, NY: McGraw-Hill, 1982), 84.

[11] Judith Orasanu and Terry Connolly, "The Reinvention of Decision Making," in *Decision Making in Action: Models and Methods*, eds. Gary A. Klein et al., (Norwood, NJ: Ablex, 1993), 19.
[12] Ibid.

[13] Zeleny, *Multiple Criteria Decision Making*, 86.

[14] Orasanu and Connolly, "The Reinvention of Decision Making," 13.

[15] Beach and Lipshitz, "Why Classical Decision Theory is an Inappropriate Standard for Evaluating and Aiding Most Human Decision Making," 25.

[16] Peter Thunholm, "A New Model for Tactical Mission Planning for the Swedish Armed Forces" (paper presented at *The State of the Art and the State of the Practice*, 2006 International Command and Control Research and Technology Symposium, San Diego, 20-22 June, 2006), 2.

http://www.dodccrp.org/events/2006_CCRTS/html/papers/094.pdf (accessed October 30, 2016).

[17] Beach and Lipshitz, "Why Classical Decision Theory is an Inappropriate Standard for Evaluating and Aiding Most Human Decision Making," 25.

[18] Gary Klein, "Naturalistic Decision Making," in *Human Factors: The Journal of the Human Factors and Ergonomics Society* 50, no. 3, (June 2008), 457.

[19] Flora Carlin, "Gut Almighty: Intuition really does come from the gut," in *Psychology Today* (1 May 2007)

http://www.psychologytoday.com/articles/200704/gut-almighty (accessed October 30, 2016).

[20] Klein, "Naturalistic Decision Making," 457.

[21] Beach and Lipshitz, "Why Classical Decision Theory is an Inappropriate Standard for Evaluating and Aiding Most Human Decision Making," 20-21.

[22] Dan Ariely, *Predictably Irrational: The Hidden Forces that Shape Our Decisions*, (London: Harper Collins, 2010), xx.

[23] Beach and Lipshitz, "Why Classical Decision Theory is an Inappropriate Standard for Evaluating and Aiding Most Human Decision Making," 23.
[24] Ibid.

[25] Klein, "Naturalistic Decision Making," 457.

[26] Tim Hindle, "Herbert Simon," *The Economist Guide to*

Management Ideas and Gurus, (March 20, 2009) http://www.economist.com/node/13350892 (accessed October 30, 2016)

[27] M. S. Cohen and Raanan Lipshitz, *Three Roads to Commitment: A Trimodal Theory of Decision Making*, (Arlington, VA: Perceptronics Solutions, 2011), submitted for publication, 3. http://www.cog-tech.com/papers/Trimodal/Decision%20 Making%201%20June%202011.pdf (accessed October 30, 2016).
[28] Ibid.

[29] Ranaan Lipshitz et al., "Taking Stock of Naturalistic Decision Making," *Journal of Behavioural Science* 14, issue 5, (2001), 333.
[30] Ibid.

[31] Orasanu and Connolly,"The Reinvention of Decision Making," 7.
[32] Ibid.

[33] Ariely, *Predictably Irrational,* xxi.

[34] Orasanu and Connolly, "The Reinvention of Decision Making," 13.

[35] Klein, "Naturalistic Decision Making," 456.
[36] Ibid.

[37] Zeleny, *Multiple Criteria Decision Making*, 86.

[38] Robert L. Ramseyer, "Ethical Decision-making and the Missionary Role," *International Bulletin of Missionary Research* 6, No. 3, (July 1982), 114 - 118.

[39] Orasanu and Connolly, "The Reinvention of Decision Making," 20.

[40] Raanan Lipshitz, "Converging Themes in the Study of Decision Making in Realistic Settings," in *Decision Making in Action: Models and Methods*, eds. Gary A. Klein et al., (Norwood, NJ: Ablex, 1993), 103.

[41] Klein, "Naturalistic Decision Making," 457-458.

[42] Ibid.

[43] Ibid., 458.

[44] Orasanu and Connolly,"The Reinvention of Decision Making," 6.

[45] Klein, "Naturalistic Decision Making," 457.

[46] Lipshitz et al., "Taking Stock of Naturalistic Decision Making," 333.

[47] Flora, "Gut Almighty".

[48] A. S. D'Aprix, "Ethical decision-making models: A two-phase study," (2005), quoted in Joe W. Cotter and Toni B. Greif, "Ethical decision-making in a fast changing world," *International Journal of Business Research* 7, Issue 5, (September 2007), http://www.freepatentsonline.com/article/International-Journal-Business-Research/178945807.html (accessed October 30, 2016)

[49] Ibid.

[50] Steven B. Sample, *The Contrarian's Guide to Leadership,* (San Francisco, CA: Jossey-Bass, 2003), 86.

[51] S.G. Scott and R.A. Bruce, "Decision-making style: The development and assessment of a new measure." (1995): 818–831, quoted in Muhammad Naveed Riaz and M. Anis-Ul-Haqu, "Leadership styles as predictors of decision making styles," in *African Journal of Business Management* 6, issue 15, (18 April 2012), 5227. http://www.academicjournals.org/AJBM/PDF/pdf2012/18April/Riaz%20and%20Haque.pdf (accessed July 20, 2012).

[52] Orasanu and Connolly, "The Reinvention of Decision Making," 19.

[53] Ibid., 20.

[54] Klein, "Naturalistic Decision Making," 457.

[55] Cohen and Lipshitz, *Three Roads to Commitment*, 5.

[56] Peter Thunholm, "A New Model for Tactical Mission Planning for the Swedish Armed Forces," 2.

[57] Klein, "Naturalistic Decision Making," 456.

[58] Cohen and Lipshitz, *Three Roads to Commitment,* 6.

[59] Gary A. Klein, "A Recognition-Primed Decision (RPD) Model of Rapid Decision Making," in *Decision Making in Action: Models and Methods*, eds. Gary A. Klein et al., (Norwood, NJ: Ablex, 1993), 146.

[60] Emergency Planning College (unknown presenter). "Defensible Decisions," Presentation given at *Tactical Leadership in Emergency Management*, United Kingdom Cabinet Office Emergency Planning College, Easingwold, UK, May 26-28, 2010.

Chapter Eleven

[1] Klein, *Sources of Power*, 169.

[2] Orasanu and Connolly, "The Reinvention of Decision Making," 7.

[3] Lipshitz et al., "Taking Stock of Naturalistic Decision Making," 336.

[4] Klein, *Sources of Power*, 4.

[5] Interviewee 2, interview by author, July 24, 2012.
[6] Interviewee 1, interview by author, July 24, 2012.
[7] Interviewee 3, interview by author, July 25, 2012.
[8] Interviewee 5, interview by author, August 3, 2012.
[9] Interviewee 2, interview by author.
[10] Interviewee 3, interview by author.
[11] Interviewee 1, interview by author.
[12] Interviewee 4, interview by author, July 26, 2012.
[13] Interviewee 6, interview by author, August 13, 2012.
[14] Interviewee 8, interview by author, August 17, 2012.

Chapter Twelve

[1] Barbara Means et al., "Training Decision Makers for the Real World," 326.

[2] Ibid., 308.

[3] Peter Thunholm, "A New Model for Tactical Mission Planning for the Swedish Armed Forces."

[4] F. Andrews, "Management: How a Boss Works in Calculated Chaos" (1976), quoted in Henry Mintzberg, *The Rise and Fall of Strategic Planning*, (Harlow: Pearson Education, 2000), 244.

[5] Henry Mintzberg, *The Rise and Fall of Strategic Planning*, (Harlow: Pearson Education, 2000), 244.

[6] Barbara Means et al., "Training Decision Makers for the Real World," 320.

[7] Ibid., 314.

[8] Ibid.

[9] Ibid., 315.

[10] Ibid.

[11] Sample, *The Contrarian's Guide to Leadership*, 7.

[12] Mary T. Lederleitner, *Cross-cultural partnerships: Navigating the Complexities of Money and Mission*, (Downer's Grove, Il: IVP, 2010), 113.

Appendix A: Corruption Response Scale quick guide

Judging an individual or organisation's place on the Corruption Response Scale is a subjective exercise. The main purpose of the scale is to give an approximate value, to permit individuals to make rapid assessments of potential conflicts before they arise. Nonetheless, a simple questionnaire is given below to help new users of the scale understand where they, their colleagues, and their organisations may lie.

To calculate your position on the Corruption Response Scale, go through the three questions on the following pages, working out your most likely position on each. Then:

1. add your three answers together;
2. divide the total answer by 3;
3. and round up or down to the nearest number

This number is your approximate position on the Corruption Response Scale.

Question 1:

Would you ever make an undocumented payment (eg Christmas tip to Postman)	→	NO	→	[1]
possibly ↓				
If the nature of your relationship with the recipient or the norms of culture encouraged it (eg tip to a waiter or baggage attendant)	→	occasionally	→	[2]
	→	sometimes	→	[3]
often ↓				
Are you likely to pay or tip in advance in order to get good service	→	NO	→	[4]
yes ↓				
Would you strongly and proactively encourage your colleagues to follow your approach?	→	NO	→	[5]
yes ↓				
Would you continue even if the messages in society are against this type of payment?	→	NO	→	[6]
	→	YES	→	[7]

Question 2:

Would you ever make a payment in order to gain a special advantage…	→	NO	→	[1]
possibly	↓			
If the payment is undocumented and no receipt given?	→	NO	→	[2]
	→	occasionally	→	[3]
sometimes	↓			
If the scale of the payment doesn't lead to significant financial or time savings elsewhere	→	NO	→	[4]
sometimes	↓			
If you know that your actions cause others greater delay?	→	NO	→	[5]
sometimes	↓			
If the messages in society are against this type of payment?	→	NO	→	[6]
	→	YES	→	[7]

Question 3:

Would you ever make an undocumented payment in order to allow an important activity to take place?		→	NO	→	[1]
possibly	↓				
Even if you thought it would be hard to justify to others		→	NO	→	[2]
		→	occasionally	→	[3]
sometimes	↓				
Even if you knew it caused others greater challenges		→	NO	→	[4]
sometimes	↓				
Even if it was just for your personal convenience or benefit		→	NO	→	[5]
sometimes	↓				
Even if the messages in society are against this type of payment?		→	NO	→	[6]
		→	YES	→	[7]

ABOUT THE AUTHOR

John Tipper's involvement in disaster response has seen him spend extended periods of time in some of the world's more troubled spots. He lived in South Sudan throughout its six year period of semi-autonomy, and has been based in the Middle East for the past four years. Along the way he has developed a deep appreciation for the role of local groups as they respond to the disasters that befall their communities. He counts himself privileged to have worked alongside and learned from such local responders in Southeast Asia and the Balkans, as well as in East Africa and the Middle East. He is married with three children.